A Garden on the Brazos

A Garden on the Brazos
Green Thoughts in a Texas Garden

Dominique Cranmer Inge

LAMAR UNIVERSITY Press

ISBN: 978-0-9850838-1-6
Library of Congress Control Number: 2013947753
Photography: Charles Inge
Manufactured in the United States of America

Lamar University Press
Beaumont, Texas

To my husband, Charles Inge,
poet, man of wisdom and love—
whose appreciation of the natural world has opened
new realms for me,

and

to the memory of my father,
Wesley Eugene Cranmer (1918-2001),
man of honor and unfailing kindness.
He instructed by gentle example.

Books from Lamar University Press

Jean Andrews, *High Tides, Low Tides: the Story of Leroy Colombo*
Alan Berecka, *With Our Baggage*
David Bowles, *Flower, Song, Dance: Aztec and Mayan Poetry*
Jeffrey Delotto, *Voices Writ in Sand*
Mimi Ferebee, *Wildfires and Atmospheric Memories*
Michelle Hartman, *Disenchanted and Disgruntled*
Gretchen Johnson, *The Joy of Deception*
Tom Mack and Andrew Geyer, editors, *A Shared Voice*
Dave Oliphant, *The Pilgrimage, Selected Poems: 1962-2012*
Harold Raley, *Louisiana Rogue*
Carol Coffee Reposa, *Underground Musicians*
Jan Seale, *Appearances*
Melvin Sterne, *The Number You Have Reached*

For more information on these and other books, go to
www.LamarUniversityPress.Org

Acknowledgments

In retrospect this book has been composting for many years. The encouragement and support of certain individuals served as catalysts for bringing it to a finished state.

I owe the greatest debt of gratitude to Judy Barrett, editor of *Homegrown: Good Sense Organic Gardening* (www. HomegrownTexas. com). In 1997 she took a chance on me as an aspiring writer and, in effect, launched my writing career. Our creative association spanned a decade and a half, and our resulting friendship continues to this day. It has been a meaningful journey, and I am deeply grateful for the opportunities presented along the way.

I offer my sincere gratitude to poet and friend Sherry Craven who first suggested the idea for this book. And it was her gift to me of a treasured volume by former U. S. Poet Laureate Stanley Kunitz that furnished my book's epigraph.

A writer will know no better friend than Jerry Craven. A self-described "literary lunatic," he has deployed his skills and tireless energies to teaching, writing, editing, and publishing countless writers through his Ink Brush Press, the online *Amarillo Bay*, and Lamar University Press. I earnestly hope he understands the full measure of my appreciation for his thoughtful guidance, and for asking me to pursue this project.

I wish to record my thanks to Marilyn Robitaille and Moumin Quazi, both educators at Tarleton State University in Stephenville, Texas. They also co-edit Tarleton's exceptional anthology, the *Langdon Review of the Arts in Texas*, a companion piece to the stimulating annual Langdon Weekend writers' conference they organize in Granbury, Texas. Volume 2 of the *Langdon Review* (2005-2006) contains my essay, *The Making of a Texas Garden or, Survival of the Fittest*, from which I drew portions of the introduction to this book. This small tribute to Marilyn's and Moumin's achievements extends to recognizing that through them I became acquainted with Sherry and Jerry Craven.

A garden does not make itself, and we here at the Brazos House rely on the essential organic horticultural services of Mike Hanley to tend to garden needs. He arrives for work each day invariably cheerful and optimistic. His integrity, work ethic, and sound advice have permitted us to work together as a team for almost twenty years. Moreover, he knows the identity and life cycle of just about every bug on the planet.

I am fortunate to have had the encouragement of my mother, Arlette Cranmer, and my late father, Wesley Cranmer. They always read and commented on my writing and most generously presented me with the four-volume *Royal Horticultural Society Dictionary of Gardening* that has proved an indispensable reference. It would have pleased my father to see this book come to fruition, and for that reason I offer the shared dedication in his memory.

I could not have written the essays contained herein without the sustained help and encouragement from my husband, Charles Inge. His observations of the natural world, our conversations about plants and our gardens, his intelligent editing of my writing—all combine to have me believe that, in many ways, he is the co-author of this book.

The garden isn't, at its best, designed for admiration or praise; it leads to an appreciation of the natural universe, and to a meditation on the connection between the self and the rest of the natural universe. And this can come not only from the single flower in its extravagant beauty, but in the consideration of the harmony established among all aspects of the garden's form.

—Stanley Kunitz, *The Wild Braid: A Poet Reflects on a Century in the Garden*

CONTENTS

Chapter 4: Seasons in the Garden

Chapter 5: Plant Nature and Nurture

Chapter 6: Garden Books

Chapter 7: Plant Apologia

Chapter 8: Vegetable Favorites

Chapter 9: Garden Dyspepsia

Chapter 10: Garden Lessons

Chapter 11: In Memoriae

Chapter 12: Garden Variety

Chapter 13: Garden Mystique

Garden Photographs

Introduction

A cauliflower is a cabbage with a college education.
—Mark Twain

In a way my love of gardening all started with trees and watercress at the Inge family farm near McKinney, Texas. Actually though, the groundwork already existed long before my experiences there, but had lain dormant for many years.

I grew up in a bilingual household speaking French to my French-born mother, and Southern English to my American father. We lived in Atlanta, Georgia, that verdant city of tall pine trees, dogwoods, and bell-skirted magnolias. Childhood years were divided between Atlanta and the shores of the Mediterranean where we enjoyed extended stays to visit my mother's family. Since my parents both had professional careers, they had neither the time nor the inclination for gardening much beyond keeping the home place tidy, mowing the lawn, clipping the hedges, and raking leaves and pine straw when necessary. Thus, for me the natural world was enjoyed rather remotely, a blend of what I saw in other people's gardens on both sides of the Atlantic: a confection of banks of azaleas, hydrangeas, Georgia peaches, and magnolia blossoms while we were Stateside, together with the lush landscapes of olive groves, vineyards, lavender fields, and potted geraniums sitting pertly on windowsills in the charming villages of Provence.

Because previous to my arrival in Texas I had never put shovel to ground, perhaps it is not surprising that I came to the Lone Star State with certain preconceived ideas about landscapes and gardening. Texas's reputation for flatness, dryness, and cactus notwithstanding, in my mind's eye all landscapes were expected to be verdant, and all gardens expected to be ever-blooming; in other words, all gardens were expected to be cottage gardens. Imagine my surprise in the middle of a scorching summer to discover dried-up lawns, prickly pear cactus with dangerous spines, scrubby trees, armadillos, rattlesnakes, and monster pickup trucks that people parked in their front yards. Such a naïve newcomer was I.

However, I soon enough discovered those mature neighborhoods of Dallas with expanses of deep lawns and majestic live oak and pecan trees so reminiscent of Atlanta. And thankfully, after Charles and I met and married, his profound appreciation for the natural world began to exert its gentle influence. Together we continued his family's tradition of weekend visits to the farm and began to experiment with growing vegetables and cultivating fruit trees.

Which brings me back to trees and watercress. The Inge farm contained some 350 acres of mixed woods and pastures with rolling terrain, mature trees, and a spring-fed pond. Charles's knowledge of the farm's flora and fauna and how he could identify all the trees and plants that grew on the farm impressed this city girl who only knew a few trees and a slim assortment of plants by name. So I asked Charles to teach me what he knew.

Thus began my weekend tutorials as we made our walkabouts at the farm. There were the cedars that lined the drive into the property; the pomegranates, abelias, and chaste trees near the farmhouse front door; a stately pair of American elms nearby that formed a cathedral-like entry to a lower section of pasture-lawn; walnut and pecan trees; honey locust trees with the menacing thorns onto which the shrikes would impale their unfortunate prey; live oaks; wild persimmons; and cedar elms with their seasonally sticky leaves. Along a fence row, a stand of old-fashioned bearded irises bloomed in spring, sporting breathtaking bicolors of mauve and burgundy. Their beauty haunts me still.

These tutorials evolved into seminars as Charles suggested some researching to gain better understanding of particular identifying characteristics. I might have known this would lead to a testing of my newfound knowledge, for sometimes he would catch me off guard in the middle of winter by asking me to identify a leafless tree by its *bark* alone. Happily, this challenging immersion into Texas botanica stirred what has become an enduring enthusiasm for botanical research.

The watercress holds another story. With my curiosity about such matters piqued, one Saturday morning, on hearing a radio personality report finding watercress at the edge of a pond in Salado, Texas and detailing the particular conditions for its growth, it occurred to me that we had those same conditions up at the farm: a spring-fed pond, dappled light, and a muddy bank. Eager for experimentation, I purchased several packets of seed, but was crestfallen by the minuscule size of the seeds. In the mistaken belief that the more the better, I broadcast the entire contents of all the packets around the edges of the farm pond. To our delight emergence occurred quickly and within a short time we had fresh watercress, considerably more than enough to share with family and friends.

My more-is-better theory actually worked in a perverse way because before long the watercress became so abundant it began to choke off the stream that fed the pond. This new challenge required some problem solving, so we devised a method of harvesting and preserving the watercress in plastic bags partially filled with some of the spring water; refrigerated in this way, the watercress could keep for many days. However, being only weekend farmers it became increasingly difficult to stay ahead with the harvesting.

One day, while shopping at a Dallas grocery chain, we mentioned our spring-fresh watercress to the produce manager. He brightened at our enthusiastic report and asked if we would be willing to supply the chain store's warehouse. We demurred at the thought of the intensive labor this would require. Nevertheless, the experience taught me some important lessons in plant cultivation.

Eventually the farm was sold, and in 1990 Charles and I purchased our first parcel of land in Granbury, Texas. Situated on a bluff near the town's historic square and overlooking Lake Granbury (formed from impounding this section of the Brazos River in the late 1960s) the property was improved with a delightful little stone, weekend getaway house. We intended using it only on weekends since Dallas remained our primary home then. Within a year of acquiring the place we called our Brazos House, we purchased an adjoining lot to the west. Although it had great potential, this new property had been neglected for a long while and would require a lot of work.

Having only weekends available to work on the property, it soon became apparent that Charles and I could not manage extensive gardening and beautification improvements by ourselves. Fortunately, Mike Hanley answered our newspaper advertisement for "organic garden help." Mike turned out to be the perfect team member for the challenges we faced, for he brought horticultural knowledge based on organic methods, practical ideas, and a sound work ethic to our numerous work projects. With Mike's help we were able to accelerate improvements.

Following the initial cleanup, although the place was ripe for the horticultural enhancements we had envisioned, we decided early on to resist planting anything until we had first acquainted ourselves more fully with our new surroundings and its denizens, so we spent many hours probing, watching, and examining the property. The unusual inhabitants of the animal, vegetable, and mineral kingdoms aroused our curiosity and sent us to references in search of their identity.

At times my enthusiasm for the discovery of new plants and flowers defied all reason as I applied myself to the study of horticulture by researching all kinds of plants, trees, wildflowers, vegetables, and roses. This energetic study included making a real effort to learn and remember the scientific names in addition to the local popular ones. In fact, I was becoming an autodidact.

Examining countless garden catalogs and books on garden design that pictured idyllic settings inspired us to attempt the same. And William Welch's book *Antique Roses for the South* was the tipping point. Antique roses (usually defined as roses introduced before 1867 when the first Hybrid Tea rose was introduced) seemed to possess charm, beauty, and fragrance in addition to hardiness. They also have compelling histories and jawbreaking names—many of them in French—two things an autodidact cannot resist with the French part being especially meaningful to me. So we began a program of planting antique roses in many spots about the place: on the fence lines, in the courtyards, and on the hillside. The roses were chosen for suitability to the Granbury area and to the specific sites.

A number of years later when the Methodist church downtown moved to a new location north of town, we expanded the property again by purchasing one of their overflow parking lots which adjoined our north line. The remedial work here would prove even more challenging than the initial development of the first expansion and the overall improvement of the Brazos House property.

For more than twenty-two years now we have continued to work with our gardens. During this time we have built a new home on the property and become permanent Granbury residents. Ever mindful of the challenges caused by our alkaline soil, high winds, and statewide drought conditions, we grow roses, vegetables, fruit trees, and native plants organically along the shores of Lake Granbury.

Perhaps it was the blend of botanical discoveries and horticultural challenges that prompted me to begin writing about our experiences. By 1997 I had already submitted a couple of articles to Judy Barrett when she was editing *The New Garden Journal*, then a companion magazine to a PBS television series *The New Garden*. She published these articles, and in 1998 asked me to write a bimonthly column for her forthcoming publication, *Homegrown: Good Sense Organic Gardening*.

This timing proved ideal for I was eager to chronicle our successes and failures and to record a bit of what I had learned through research. These vignettes first appeared in a column called "Notes from the Brazos," and continued for thirteen years until *Homegrown* ceased publication in 2010 (it resumed publication on line at www.HomegrownTexas.com).

This book is a selection of vignettes taken from those columns, somewhat revised and edited for the purposes here. They were a joy to research and write, with Judy Barrett such a congenial editor to work with over the years. Then, as now, I have made every effort at accuracy, so if any errors are found here the responsibility is mine and mine alone.

Today, tempered by more than twenty-two years of gardening experience at our Brazos House home and gardens we are trying to allow the gardens to mature naturally, making adjustments here and there, but without feeling the compulsion to exert as much control as once we did. Mother Nature is, after all, *the* alpha female in this world, and acknowledging her dominant role will allow us all to get along much better in our gardening efforts.

Visitors to the Brazos House grounds have been generous in their praise, but the remark I value most came from a large, shy, burly man who said he liked coming to this place "because everything looks so natural." Gardening anywhere requires human intervention, but if we can strike a balance by learning to intervene without becoming interlopers, then I shall feel gratified.

Dominique Cranmer Inge
Granbury, Texas

Chapter 1
Flower Portraits and Provenance

A Gardener's Serendipity: The Moonflower

Serendipity is one of gardening's unproclaimed joys. Often such fortuitous discoveries, though sometimes small or insignificant, will brighten our day, making us cry out with a child's delight. Like the little potted plant stumbled over in the nursery aisle, just perfect for that vacant spot in the garden. Or perhaps a tomato bush, heavy with plump fruit, found volunteering at the base of a hollyhock. Or, an effective fertilizer formula, accidentally developed by a felicitous blending of exotic ingredients. Then there are seed packets, casually plucked from the shelves of a grocery store kiosk, examined for suitability and tossed in the shopping cart. This is how I found the moonflower.

The full, open face of a moonflower's creamy blossom appeared on the seed envelope like a 1930s soft-focus picture of a Hollywood star. Written beneath the floral silver screen portrait were words promising "delicious fragrance," and "huge white blossoms open at dusk." A fanciful mind might read them as the celebrity's imaginary personality traits leaving us, well, slightly breathless, if only for an instant.

Noted for their extraordinary fragrance, nocturnal blooming, and vigorous growth, moonflowers (also called moonvines) are relatives of the common morning glory and the sweet potato. As a member of the Convol-vulaceae family, the moonflower's twining growth habit suggests its current scientific name: *Ipomoea alba*, from the Greek *ips* (worm) and *homoios* (resembling). But this is just character acting for the moonflower; like any superstar, the moonflower sometimes bears another stage name,

Calonyction aculeatum (from Greek *kalos*, meaning "beautiful," and *nyktos*, meaning "night").

Moonflowers are meant for nightlife: they are said to "bloom by the moon and close by the sun." They open in late afternoon, continue blooming throughout the evening, and then close by mid-morning. Flowers remain open for longer periods on overcast days or when temperatures cool.

Native to the tropics, moonflowers are perennials in USDA Zones 9 and 10, annuals elsewhere. They are vigorous growers (reaching 10 to 20 feet in a season) and require full sun to very light shade. Moonflowers propagate easily from seeds, which look like small chickpeas. Soak the seed overnight first, then sow singly in peat pots to avoid disturbing roots. They need a long growing season and heat of the summer to bloom, so seed should be started about six to eight weeks before transplanting, after danger of frost. Flowering lasts from summer through fall.

Taking complementary bloom cycles into account, some gardeners pair morning glories with moonflowers, thereby enjoying an almost continuous floral show. Contrasted with their large, glossy, heart-shaped leaves, moonflowers are as white and luscious as Devon cream. Delicately embossed at the blossom's center is a starfish pattern, giving the trumpet-shaped flower a suppleness most graceful in a lunar glow. Measuring four to six inches across, many fully opened blossoms are large as dessert plates. They are soft, cool, and silken to the touch. Yet for all their fragile beauty they do not seem to mind human contact. Moonflowers, after all, are meant to be applauded, possessed by admiring fans.

Often the moonflower is embraced by one of its insect fans, the spectacular sphinx moth. Emerging only at twilight, the moth hovers like a hummingbird while it plunges its tapered proboscis into the flower's heart. The blossom shudders momentarily and then resumes its serene pose in the lunar limelight. The hope of discovering a newly opened moonflower being visited by a sphinx moth may be reason enough to delay bedtime for any gardening fan.

Feeding insects are not the only ones attracted by the moonflower's lavish fragrance. Evening strollers catch whiffs of what might be described as an exotic blend of orange blossom, baby powder, and cloves as the moonflower casts its scent. Awaiting those luxuriant blooms is like waiting for a star herself to arrive on opening night. Steve Bender, in his book *Passalong Plants,* relates the story of a neighbor whose friends gathered punctually at 5 o'clock each afternoon to watch the blooming of her moonflower. "They'd always arrive at the same time, trying to time it," she says. "We could tell which blooms were about to open, because they'd start to quiver. They were quick—turn your back and you'd miss it." Take heed, paparazzi.

Moonflowers offer an unsurpassed floral extravaganza. On a moonlit night it is a blockbuster performance. The heady scent might calm the ill-tempered child, make rage fall away from an irascible neighbor, refine an old codger, or provide an effective soporific for the insomniac.

The German poet Goethe writes, "The flower is a leaf mad with love." He was speaking of the luminous moonflower, no doubt.

Blazing Heirlooms: The Oxblood Lily

A signal that at last summer has transitioned into fall comes each year in our Brazos House gardens in the form of the striking oxblood lily. Its other common name, "schoolhouse lily," presumably was bestowed because it may have been planted frequently outside rural schoolhouses, or perhaps because its bloom cycle coincides with the beginning of school in autumn. No wonder then that masses of these compact, flaming showstoppers bring to mind elementary school children during a fire drill, standing close and alert outside the school building.

"Oxblood" aptly describes the intensity of the flower's color. Botanically related to amaryllis, the oxblood lily's current scientific name, *Rhodophiala bifida*, helps form a picture of its color and shape: *rhodon* from the Greek red or rose, the Latin words *phiala* meaning bowl or drinking vessel, and *bifida* meaning cleft or forked. Whether seen from near or far, the vivid, funnel-shaped, cleft flowers glow atop slender, bright green stalks. Standing erect, about 12" tall, they nod slightly, grouped in clusters, with heads turned this way and that.

Flowers emerge from bulbs in late summer to early fall, usually following a rain. The fact that they bloom long before the shiny, strap-like leaves appear makes for a perennial surprise. They seem to have popped up overnight, causing exclamations of delight and feelings of relief in this first notice that cooler weather now is on its way.

Oxblood lilies are genuine heirlooms, distributed widely within the Southern states. Native to Argentina and Uruguay, they are found most commonly in the central Texas communities settled by German

9

immigrants, one of whom, botanist Peter Heinrich Oberwetter, is credited with introducing oxblood lilies to America sometime after the Civil War and during the period he lived in Austin, from about 1900 until 1915.

Valued for their beauty and hardiness, oxblood lilies have passed to successive generations. In his informative book *Garden Bulbs for the South* Scott Ogden states why they have endured: "No other Southern bulb can match the fierce vigor, tenacity, and adaptability of the oxblood lily. Whether planted on worn-out gumbo clay or on impoverished sand, the long-necked black bulbs make themselves at home."

Easy to cultivate for novice or expert gardeners, oxblood lilies grow in full sun to part shade, tolerate a variety of soils, and multiply quickly. Their roots penetrate deep into the ground. The mother bulb sends out smaller offsets, the new bulbs forming "a curious twisting pattern," says Ogden, allowing the lilies to increase into clumps.

Remarkably, these resilient bulbs can withstand disturbance even during their blooming season, as personal experience attests. One year, in an effort to save our lilies from a construction project, we took a deep breath, dug them up, heeled them in, and then replanted in a safer spot sometime later. Next season, without missing a beat, they bloomed in their new location, looking as if they had grown there always.

Gardeners probably will not find oxblood lilies in nurseries or garden centers. If they can be found commercially at all, they will be available most likely through bulb or heirloom plant specialists. Their price will be dear, but these plants are worth it. Acquiring them in a more personal way, by sharing through family or friends, or discovering a clump on your own homestead as we did, seems more authentic.

If you are fortunate enough to possess oxblood lilies, recognize their value by passing some on to keep the gene pool alive. Then, next school season your beneficiaries, in turn, probably will report with delight how those same schoolhouse lilies ignited their own gardens with radiant blooms.

Paean for Pansies

Despite our disinclination to plant annuals at the turn of every season, pansies are a notable exception in our mostly perennial gardens. Our reservations concerning annuals are rooted in reasons ranging from the costs associated with purchasing multiple flats of bedding plants to the logistics of transportation and mass placement, and the nuisance of digging up plants from the previous season for replacement with new ones that, in turn, must be pulled up and consigned to the compost heap. This endless cycle perpetuates itself season after season.

However, pansies offer too perfect an excuse to break our own rules for their flowers are so pert and charming having the effect of giving a whole garden an instant lift by providing intensely colorful contrast to gray days of late fall or winter. And the velvety luxuriance of their blooms softens otherwise stark landscapes.

The care and feeding of pansies also can happily occupy the otherwise restless gardener during a dormant season. Occasionally deadheading spent flowers to tidy their appearance and encourage more blooms, as well as feeding with measured amounts of blood meal or coffee grounds around the base of the plants can serve to calm fidgety green thumbs when there's nothing much else in bloom. They also buoy the gardener's flagging spirit in the cooler months by supplying instant cheer with blossoms that often suggest jovial faces. Massed together, these flowery faces seem to combine into an imaginary audience, trembling with enthusiasm while swaying in a cool, gentle breeze.

Pansies are members of the well-known genus *Viola*. For this reason it is almost impossible to talk about the modern, large-flowered garden pansy—first developed in England about 1810 to 1813—without also mentioning its important ancestor, *Viola tricolor*, commonly known in the US as johnny-jump-up, owing to its habit of catapulting its seeds so that new plants spring up where least expected.

A native of Europe and discovered as early as 1600, *V. tricolor* has diminutive flowers in appealing combinations of yellow, blue, violet, and white. These flowers, often referred to as pansies, derive their name from the French word for thoughts or, *pensées*, presumably because the flowers often look like faces in contemplation. The Victorians extended this notion to a high art in their secret language of flowers by ascribing to pansies sentiments such as "Think of me," or "You occupy my thoughts."

Pansies and *V. tricolor* share myriad other common names such as hearts-ease, ladys'-delight, forget-me-not, love-in-idleness, butterfly violet, merit-neglected, three faces-under-a-hood, variegated violet, none-so-pretty, winged violet, field pansy, godfathers-and-godmothers, jack-jump-up-and-kiss-me, kit-run-in-the-fields, meet-me-in-the-entry, and kiss-her-in-the-buttery.

With such a store of witty and endearing names it is not surprising that pansies are closely associated with love. The origins of this association go back at least to Ancient Greece. The word violet, from Greek *Ion*, contains the name of a young girl whom the god Zeus loved. Wanting to protect Io from his jealous wife, Hera, he changed the girl into a heifer, placing her within a field of violets, where she might eat. Shakespeare immortalizes the flowers in *Midsummer Night's Dream* as "love-in-idleness," a name still used in the Stratford-upon-Avon locality. And in *Twelfth Night* it is his central character, Viola, who embodies the virtues of reason, intelligence, and mature love.

Among the historical figures it was Napoleon who, when exiled to Elba, promised his Empress Josephine that he would "return with violets."Although Napoleon was said to have sometimes neglected Josephine's merits, he always knew there was none so pretty as she. Perhaps Napoleon had in mind to announce his arrival by a message of flowers "Meet-Me-in-the-Entry." Yet by the time he did return with his bouquet of violets, his beloved Josephine had died.

Paperwhites for a New Year

Strolls through the gardens in wintertime tend to be shorter ones than those of warmer months. Dormant grass, pale skies, and bare tree branches combine to form monochrome compositions that lessen one's spirits and the desire for walks, if it were not for the uplifting, vibrant colors of pyracantha and nandina berries, and the colored hips of climbing roses anchored along the fences.

But venturing outdoors in winter offers other rewards as well, such as paperwhite narcissus blooming in pert clumps at the base of frost-covered benches. Creamy white, fragrant blossoms please the eyes and tantalize the nose, their charm seeming to banish the cold long enough for chill fingers to pluck a few stems for bringing indoors. The intense musky fragrance fills the nostrils so agreeably that any impatience caused earlier by wrestling to reattach a winterized hose to an exterior faucet instantly melts away.

The botanical name for paperwhites, *Narcissus papyraceus*, has its origins in Greek mythology. Narcissus was a handsome young man, incapable of feelings of love for anyone other than himself. The hapless nymph, Echo, fell in love with him, and when Narcissus spurned her, she withdrew to a mountain cave. She died there longing for the handsome youth, leaving only her voice echoing in the mountains. One day Narcissus paused in the woods to drink from a pool, and on seeing his own reflection in the water, fell in love with it. Reaching into the pool to possess his own image, he fell in and drowned. When wood nymphs came in search of his body, they found nothing but a beautiful, fragrant flower with white petals, the narcissus. Hence, in the language of the sentiment of flowers made so popular by Victorians, the narcissus is associated with egotism and excessive self-love.

Narcissus and daffodil often are treated as synonymous, and paperwhites usually are classed as cultivars of the Tazetta daffodil group. In his book *Garden Bulbs for the South* Scott Ogden relates that "the specific epithet, *tazetta*, originates from an Italian term for the 'little cups,' or coronas, of the blossoms, which are centered like e[s]presso mugs in the elfin saucers formed by the surrounding petals."

Native to the Mediterranean region, these flowers grow to about 15 inches tall with pointed petals and orange-yellow stamens within a frilled corona. *Papyraceus* refers, of course, to papyrus, or the paper-like whiteness of the petals.

Paperwhites make elegant ornamental displays when brought to bloom indoors. Unlike many other bulbs, they do not need a chilling period or fertilizer. Their ease of growing adds to their appeal. They can be grown in shallow containers filled with soil, gravel, sand, or marbles, with water enough for moisture. If grown in glass containers filled with pebbles, their roots show through the glass as they take hold, growing like slender, white filaments around the pebbles.

The Chinese grow paperwhites in pots to celebrate each New Year. What a charming idea—to begin each year afresh, perfumed with fragrant, lovely winter flowers.

Indoor Spectacular: Forsythia, Witch Hazel, Flowering Quince

Often during the first months of the year magazines appear filled with glossy photos of perfect winter-blooming plants. Amaryllis or paperwhite narcissi emerging from pots or elegant vases are arranged with Zen-like artistry to showcase their spectacular blooms. For our area of North Central Texas, there will be pictures of deep planting beds containing cool-season annuals such as pansies, or pert cool-climate perennials used as annuals such as English daisy and English primrose. Sweet peas may grace the pages of garden magazines for our area at about this time, showing how to add color and some vertical interest to an otherwise colorless outdoor palette.

Sometimes compelling photos will depict the forced blooms of forsythia, witch hazel, and flowering quince. Many years ago I tore out the entire center section of a national gardening magazine containing photos and an article about these dramatic winter blooms. Though I intended keeping the section for future ready-reference, it has long since disappeared. Yet the photographs of those brilliant, wild-looking blooms gathered and placed in tall vases set indoors in front of windows framing a winter landscape will stay with me forever.

Forsythia was named for 18th century Scottish botanist and horticulturalist William Forsyth, a royal head gardener and who became one of the founding members of the Horticultural Society of London, later known as the Royal Horticultural Society. First introduced from China and Japan, in the nineteenth century to Western gardens, forsythia has remained a popular shrub valued for its radiant yellow or gold blossoms which occur usually in late winter in our area of Texas. Deciduous (sometimes semi-evergreen), they are of medium height at 6 to 10 feet tall with soft-wooded stems branching from the ground. They are frost hardy in zones 5 to 9, and make excellent cut flowers when in full bloom. Stems containing flowers at bud stage may be brought indoors for bloom forcing.

Witch hazel comes from East Asia. It is a deciduous, upright, open shrub or small tree that grows 10 to 15 feet tall, preferring sunny spots, and hardy in zones 4 to 9. Its fragrant flowers vary in color from light yellow to deep orange depending on cultivar, and in mid to late winter the flowering branches may be cut for indoor decoration. The twisted, spidery-looking flowers clustered on bare branches make interesting and unusual arrangements. Witch hazel (*Hamamelis*) twigs have been used for water divining, perhaps because the Old English word "witch" means pliant branches. Witch hazel extracts have also been used in medicine.

Flowering quince (*Chaenomeles speciosa*), originating in China, Japan, and Korea, is another precocious bloomer. Its stems form a dense thicket growing into a shrub 5 to 10 feet tall that can adapt to a range of garden conditions, but prefers sunny spots with well-drained soil. Its flowers may be red, pink, coral, or yellow, appearing on thorny branches in late winter or earliest spring. Like forsythia and witch hazel, the budded stems may be brought indoors for forcing into wonderful floral displays. Left outside, the flowers are followed in summer by fruits that may be eaten alone, or made into jams or jellies.

We have one plant each of forsythia, witch hazel, and flowering quince in our gardens. Unfortunately, they do not make optimum displays since for a long while now they have been shaded by the larger shrubs and trees surrounding them. But occasionally I enjoy collecting some of their branches to bring indoors to see if they come ablaze with colors like the spectacular photos I have remembered so well.

Garden Wows: Iris

Few flowers can prompt more wows in a garden than irises. Even fewer can meet multiple standards of excellence such as spectacular appearance, variety of color and species, fragrance, perennial low maintenance, disease resistance, ready availability, suitability for most climates, usefulness as cut flowers, rich in history and lore, and interesting to grow for novice and seasoned gardener alike.

At first blush such description may read something like the over-blown self-images found in personal column ads, but in this case the qualities of iris are not exaggeration. Iris merits consistent top marks every time.

Irises enhance spring days with splendor in our Brazos House gardens when they bloom March to April. Sometimes called sword lilies, they emerge from within a fan of flat, sword-like leaves. Multiple, tightly coiled cones rise on stems sometimes 36" to 42" high. Over several weeks the flowers unfurl in an array of breathtaking colors. As each delicate petal unfolds it flutters on a passing breeze, evoking the soft grace of a chiffon scarf.

Once spent, the veined petals of the iris begin to resemble the texture and translucency of lettuce leaves. Fading, they recede into a small, moist fist, a kind of reverse blooming. The papery calyx, appearing at first like a sling to support each budding flower, in its final stage looks more like a mummy's sheath, falling away casually from the stem.

These luscious flowers derive their name from Iris, goddess of clas-sical mythology and messenger of the gods. As she soared to the heavens she would leave a rainbow in her path. Thus, the ancient Greeks and

Garden Wows
Irises

Romans associated her with the spirit of the rainbow, a beautiful link between Earth and other worlds. Her name also survives to identify the colored portion of the eye, the iris, as well as in the word "iridescent."

There are hundreds of species of the genus *Iris* and related genera, classified into a complex system of subgenera, sections, subsections, and series—a discussion best left to experts in taxonomy. Most home gardeners distinguish between bulbous irises and rhizomatous irises. The well-known Dutch irises belong to the bulbous group as they are planted from bulbs. The bearded, beardless, and crested irises belong to the rhizomatous group, meaning that they are planted from rhizomes, a long, leathery root.

Some terminology might be helpful to gardeners wishing to order their bearded irises from catalogs where they are most often described by their parts. The three central upright petals, touching together like praying hands, are called standards; the three lower petals, sweeping downward, are known as falls. Rows of hairs, or "beards" in the center of the falls give the bearded group its name. Irises of a single color are called selfs; bi-tone irises have falls and standards of different colors.

While iris taxonomy may be fiendishly complex, their cultivation is simplicity itself. Scores of books and articles exist on the subject, and each section of the country may require different planting and fertilizing methods. In general, transplanting around Labor Day has proven to be a good time for our bearded irises. We fertilize three times with a light dusting of bone meal around Valentine's Day (about six weeks before expected blooming), after blooming (usually in May), then again at trans-planting time. Irises can suffer from overcrowding so when established beds become matted (three to five years), dig them up, divide the rhizomes, discard any damaged ones, then transplant. Irises make desirable gifts for gardening friends so division time is an opportunity to share. This also helps to keep the gene pool alive.

Irises make spectacular cut flowers, filling the room with a rich perfume. Fresh blossoms can last several days. Monitor the arrangement daily and cut any spent flowers before they reach the moist, closed stage. Wait too long and they collapse, dripping an indelible inky residue on a prized table or rug.

With minimal effort irises will reward busy gardeners each spring with their own private garden rainbows—indoors or out—wowing admirers along the way.

Chapter 2
In Love with Spring

Poppies

Spring brings poppies. The arresting frankness of their blossoms fills the eye and fixes the attention, much like a lead actor commanding the stage. Surrounding flowers or vegetation, no matter how strong or handsome, recede into the background when in the company of poppies, becoming supporting actors, destined to play only the secondary roles on a garden stage.

And why shouldn't poppies claim the limelight? Exotic and flamboyant, these lavish flowers emerge in mid to late April (in our area), manifesting in vivid colors that range from scarlet, crimson, and salmon, to pale pink, medium pink, deep rose, saffron, and white.

A poppy's crepe-like petals unfurl from within a green sepal gracefully bent over a slender, hairy stem. Once the sepal separates and rights itself to release the enclosed petals, they discard the sepal and open to form a delicate, fluttery bowl. Softly crinkled, the silken petals seem to take energy from the atmosphere, slowly unfolding and filling out like a butterfly freed of its chrysalis.

Soon, bees tumble in the flower cup, releasing the yellow or sometimes grayish-green pollen. By nightfall, the crinoline petals and stamens will have fallen away, leaving the pistil standing alone with a chenille-like cap. As the pistil dries, the barrel or turret-shaped enclosure opens a series of tiny apertures beneath the cap, like clerestory windows, allowing ventilation, and a means of escape for the tiny seeds within.

Dozens of species of poppies exist, but about five or six are the most common ones: *Papaver somniferum*, the notorious opium poppy, and *P. rhoeas*, the corn or "Flanders" poppy, including its "Shirley" strain, are annuals; the gorgeous *P. nudicaule*, or "Iceland" poppy, is considered a short-lived perennial, treated as an annual, while *P. orientale*, "Oriental" poppy, is a true perennial. Also, in Texas, we must not forget the wildly beautiful *P. argemone* (prickly poppy) and the intensely colored "California" poppy, *Eschscholzia californica*.

Most poppies are easy and rewarding to grow from seed. Expect best results in this area when they are direct-sown in the fall. We plant our "Shirley" poppies in October or November every year, and usually have blooms by April. The seeds are miniscule, like pepper, so a common mistake is sowing too thickly. When the seed packet says to sow thinly, it means *thinly*. Also, do not cover the seeds with too much soil; poppies need light to germinate. In disturbed ground they will self-sow, sometimes coming up in surprising places—a boon for gardeners who like a little serendipity.

Papaver means poppy in Latin. The name may allude to the milky sap found in *P. somniferum,* used in making narcotics. *Somniferum* refers to its soporific properties. Poppies have a compelling history, having inspired extravagant behavior as well as extravagant praise for millennia. Use of *P. somniferum* as a narcotic or soporific dates to ancient civilizations, to Sumerian, Assyrian, Babylonian, and Egyptian times.

The early Greeks and Romans used the poppy as a test for fidelity. A suspicious lover would place a petal on the right hand and slap it with the left. If the petal popped he was assured of a true love; if it made no sound, his beloved's faithfulness was doubtful.

As to praise, English poet Robert Browning exalts "the Poppy's red effrontery," while English art critic and tastemaker John Ruskin writes, "the poppy is painted *glass*; it never glows so brightly as when the sun shines through it. Wherever it is seen—against the light or with the light—always, it is a flame, and warms the wind like a blown ruby."

A Mother's Day Rose: "Veilchenblau"

Each year the month of May marks a special day to honor mothers, and roses from the garden help in celebrating this occasion. Most mothers would accept any flower as tribute from a child, but the rose long ago supplanted other flowers in universal appeal and importance.

My earliest association with roses centered on one called "Veilchen-blau." Although its name was unknown to my family at the time, I can remember this rose in full bloom every Mother's Day at my childhood home in Georgia. Planted at the base of the mailbox at the street curb, it entwined gracefully around the post and box, its crimson-lavender blossoms piling in extravagant mounds atop the decorative ironwork. It drew admiring comments from neighbors and passersby, and each Mother's Day my mother and my father and I would have a picture made next to Veilchenblau.

It received no special care other than perfunctory shearing to restrain its size, and occasionally receiving an accidental dose of fertilizer intended for the lawn. It required so little, yet came forth unfailingly in vigor and splendor each year.

After my parents retired and moved away, a kind neighbor recalling our affection for the Veilchenblau, sent some cuttings to my parents as a remembrance of their former neighborhood. My mother rooted these and then planted them in the yard of their new home. They flourished, and my mother, in turn, gave me cuttings from her plants. Those flourished, too, so that now there are six, mature, second-generation Veilchenblau from the original Georgia grandmother plant making spectacular displays along our fence lines and trellises here in Granbury each Mother's Day.

Veilchenblau is a favored rose in our garden not only for these sentimental associations, but also because it behaves like a well-mannered guest. It is not fussy about conditions and serves to extend the season by blooming somewhat later than many of the roses. The long graceful canes are easy to handle and have practically no thorns (prickles). The pointed leaves stay a bright green so that the foliage looks good, even shirking off occasional bouts of black spot. The clustered flower buds are neatly pointed, too, first emerging with an intense, almost fuchsia color. As they open, the flowers turn reddish-mauve with multiple tiny, layered petals, like miniature ballerina tutus, with white centers and yellow stamens. At this stage their distinctive fresh apple scent becomes strong. The blossoms then fade to a lavender-blue as they age.

Taking its name from these colors, Veilchenblau in German means "violet-blue." It was first introduced in 1909 and possesses all the admirable features of its Hybrid Multiflora class, such as ease of culture, fragrance, and myriad small blossoms. It can be trained to climb and partners well with other flowering climbers or, if given sufficient space, can ramble naturally along a fence row.

Regrettably, this rose does not make a good cut flower for almost as soon as a branch is clipped, the flower petals fall away. Moreover, Veilchenblau blooms only once; likewise, Mother's Day comes only once a year. Yet celebrating both together does makes the wait worthwhile.

"Mermaid," the Rose Rampant

Savvy gardeners know about "Mermaid." Depending on circumstances, they know this rose can be an asset, or a liability. Gardeners know that Mermaid's virtues can become its vices, its vigor transformed into invasiveness to overtake any available or unavailable space. They know that the large, yellowish-white blossoms are borne on stems that form a dense mat, sporting vicious, reverse-curved prickles (thorns) that snag and tug and tear at the least brush with them and elicit yelps of pain from even the most stoic gardeners. Thick gauntlets protecting forearms, Three Musketeers fashion, offer poor armor against this rose, for it has a formidable, practically impenetrable, natural defense system.

These same savvy gardeners know that while Mermaid may be classified among the ten best roses in Great Britain, some rosarians in the US have assigned it to the "Ten Roses Never to Plant" group. They assert its growth habits too rampant and extensive for the average home garden, that it will kill trees if left to grow in them, and that it is too tender to cultivate in northern climates. They caution its use in areas where children might play, or in situations requiring tight management or control.

Often disbelieving of the admonitions, eager novice gardeners sometimes will plant Mermaid in ill-advised areas. Then, astonished at the rose's excessive growth rate, they become alarmed, make noble attempts to subdue it, eventually warning visitors to their garden to STAY AWAY FROM THAT ROSE. At last, at the next rose society meeting they make an urgent appeal, a touching supplication for help. The wise, experienced gardeners exchange meaningful glances, bestowing rueful smiles in the direction of the supplicant. "It's been in the ground three years? Nothing you can do now," they say. "Might as well just turn the whole area over to it."

Despite its bad reputation, Mermaid is a fine old rose for the Southern garden *if* placed judiciously. Plant it near an unsightly outbuilding you may wish to camouflage, or use it to form a dense hedge in a remote area of the yard or garden so that it will attract birds or repel interlopers. Anyone caught in the tangled thicket of Mermaid likely will stay ensnared long enough for you to summon help.

English nurseryman William Paul first introduced Mermaid, a Species Hybrid rose, in 1918. It is a cross between the Macartney Rose (*Rosa bracteata)*, considered an invasive, suckering weed in Texas pasturelands, and a yellow tea rose. Such parentage explains its vigor (but without the suckering habit), and the delicate beauty of its blossoms. Each lightly fragrant, saucer-size bloom has five petals with deep golden stamens which remain on the sepals after the petals have fallen away. Bloom time is usually late spring to early summer with some repeat blooming in late summer and fall. Mermaid can be affected by hard freezes, but seems to be hardy within zone 7.

We planted the Mermaid now growing in our Brazos House garden some twenty years ago. It forms a hedge now extending 45 feet across a rail fence at the south side of the property. The sight of it in May and June amazes visitors, and they are astonished that it is a single plant. The main trunk alone is perhaps five inches in caliper.

Mike Shoup, owner of the Antique Rose Emporium in Independence, Texas, states in his book *Roses in the Southern Garden* that until he, by chance, first saw a spectacular rose later identified as Mermaid covering a chain-link fence, he had "never thought of roses as something that could endure the extremes of Texas climate without a gardener's care. Mermaid opened my eyes," he says.

Ranunculus

Gardeners hardly need wonder why most of us are "hopelessly in love with spring," borrowing a phrase from poet-philosopher George Santa-yana. Indeed, the pleasure and excitement of the sights, sounds, and smells of the season do cause us to indulge in extended wanderings through our gardens, taking in all that spring offers. Some years it is the lush yet tidy beauty of ranunculus that stirs my blood. The double or semi-double rosette blooms of *Ranunculus asiaticus* resemble miniature peonies. Formed of dense swirls, the flowers stand alone on tall stems above deeply-lobed foliage. Petals of rich, emphatic colors in yellow, red, pink, white, and purple often are edged in blushes of paler, complementary hues.

Counted among the finest of spring annuals, ranunculus offers added bonuses. Appearing often before other spring flowers, their vibrancy resonates while the gardens display little color elsewhere. Easy to grow in any sunny spot, they last longer than most tuberous annuals, and make superb cut flowers.

Ranunculus has numerous unexpected associations. As member of the Ranunculaceae or buttercup family it lists anemones, clematis, and columbines among its many cousins. And its genus name derives from Latin *rana* meaning "frog," presumably because some species grow in wet places where frogs abide. Common names for *Ranunculus asiaticus* species include buttercup as well as crowfoot, the latter perhaps alluding to their small tubers with "talons" somewhat resembling crow's claws. With a history that reaches back to ancient Turkey and the Mediterranean, they enjoyed popularity in the eighteenth century and found their way into Thomas Jefferson's planting schemes at his beloved Monticello.

Ranunculus performs best in cool, moist weather. In our area we plant in December, giving ample time to establish before the onset of the coldest weather. Though preferring sunny spots, ranunculus will tolerate a small amount of shade and provides an appealing addition to rock gardens or borders, making it ideal for small gardens. But for the best display, mass ranunculus in groups.

Soaking the tubers in root stimulant or for about thirty minutes before planting gives them a head start. Prepare a planting bed with plenty of compost, and place each tuber with the talons pointing down. Ranunculus loves water, especially in early growing stages.

With all these tasks complete, the real challenge will be stemming one's impatience while waiting for ranunculus to emerge. After what may seem like countless days of watching and waiting, the first leaves begin to appear in early February—not so long really in a gardener's world.

As ranunculus continues to develop and flower, it may become increasingly challenging to curb the excitement about its alluring displays. In the romantic tradition of the Victorians a clever way of communicating their exuberance was found when assigning to ranunculus very particular meanings: *You are radiant with charms; You are rich in attractions.* Who could express such enthusiasm in any better way than this?

Ranunculus

Cosmopolitan Cosmos

For unfailing garden allure cosmos ranks high. Profusions of large, daisy-like flowers formed of overlapping, gently serrated petals surround a raised golden center. They display a galaxy of radiant hues, and the tall, branching, feathery foliage creates a painterly, impressionistic effect worthy of any budding Monet's palette. Cosmos make gardens—and gardeners—smile.

Cosmos made me smile in girlish wonder many years ago when as a novice gardener I committed flower seed to earth for the first time. A garden primer suggested cosmos as flowers for children to grow since the flowers are practically trouble-free and germinate quickly enough to satisfy a child's attention span. These informative tips matched my situation perfectly at the time.

Yet my package of cosmos seeds contained a mystery that seemed more suitable for an adult. Rather than finding smooth, round seeds inside a plump, glossy paper packet as expected, all the cosmos seeds had settled to the bottom and were crunchy to the touch. They looked like long, thin, curved, black needles—or cat's claws. The seeds clung to the inside wrapper, requiring several peeks inside the torn packet to be sure it fully emptied.

Believing it necessary to make adjustments for the seed's size, I sowed packet after packet of "Sensation Mix" cosmos by broadcasting the seeds carelessly and everywhere in sweeping, unstudied swaths. It was simpleton's logic, that if a little is good, of course, a lot is better. The number of seeds put out that year defies estimation.

Consistent with the information supplied by the garden primer, the first seedlings emerged within three weeks. Indeed, a Lilliputian forest of medium green had sprung up almost overnight. Bear in mind that during this phase of acquiring gardening knowledge I was still struggling to learn the differences between annuals, biennials, and perennials, so the common advisory to *thin* the emerging cosmos was a concept too advanced to contemplate at the time. In fact, I did not thin. Yet the plants grew to their average height of 2 to 3 feet, flourishing in full sun.

As sometimes will happen, luck visits the beginner. In her infinite wisdom it seems Mother Nature made cosmos a gregarious flower, so crowded conditions made little difference to this cosmopolite, native to Mexico and Central America. Its name, from the Greek *kosmos*, means "orderly," "universe," "the world." Also, appropriately, it can mean ornament. Thus, my artless first efforts brought forth an exotic kind of order from chaos. The cosmos so informally planted yielded blooms positively enchanting in their simplicity and lack of pretense. Moreover, they produced in a nourishing sequence from May to November and happily reseeded with vigor.

That experiment took place many garden plots ago. Through the years and by much experience I have become a more seasoned gardener. Yet the truth is I still like to sow cosmos in the way I did that first magical year. Only difference now, however, the plantings are expanded to include whole collections of cosmos, with varieties such as "Gloria," "Daydream," "Tetra Versailles Red," "Psycho White,"the sulphurous "Klondyke," and even the dwarf varieties.

I am frankly enamored of this flower's easy manner and of the festive bouquets that attract hosts of nectar gatherers. Cosmos make the garden smile.

Papa's Favorite: The Hibiscus

Every Father's Day memories of my late father's favorite flower come to mind. He was a modest man of even temperament who taught by example, and he possessed a quiet self-assurance that drew others to him. Hibiscus was his chosen flower. That he was so attracted to it is surprising in some ways because hibiscus is anything but modest or reserved. It is self-proclaiming and showy, even when occupying space as a background plant. Its audacious blooms demand center stage in any setting, something my father never would do. Perhaps he saw in hibiscus those attributes he secretly might have wished for in himself. If the old adage is true—opposites attract—then Papa and hibiscus were indeed attracting opposites.

The hibiscus my father knew is the common tropical hibiscus, *Hibiscus rosa-sinensis*. It thrives in the warm, greenhouse climate of the island where he lived, off the Georgia coast. With its glossy, dark green foliage, and heights reaching to six feet or more, the hibiscus there are magnificent flowering shrubs sporting continuous summer blooms four to eight inches wide, ranging in color from white to pink, red, yellow, apricot, and orange. Many varieties are available, and all attract bees, butterflies, and birds. While hibiscus may be grown in our Zone 7, they require careful attention and protection from freezing.

Hibiscus is the Greek name for mallow, hence its scientific Latin family name *Malvaceae*, whose plants include hollyhock, cotton, okra, and rose of Sharon as lustrous cousins to hibiscus. This family also includes rose pavonia, Turk's cap, and winecup. Like hibiscus, they also bear elegant, ornamental flowers.

There are some 220 species of the genus *Hibiscus*. Rose mallow (*H. moscheutos*),with hybrid selections such as "Disco Belle," "Frisbee," and "Rio Carnival," offers flowers the size of dessert plates in colors ranging from red, pink, rose, to white. There is also Confederate rose (*H. mutabilis*) which can be grown like a small tree. And rose of Sharon or althea (*H. syriacus*) enjoys popularity as a sun and heat-loving shrub with conspicuous blossoms in a variety of colors. The hibiscus known as Jamaica flower (*H. sabdariffa)* is grown for its edible flowers which are used in jellies, sauces, and teas.

But back to *H. rosa-sinensis*, with its common names Chinese hibiscus, red hibiscus, and shoe flower. Shoe flower? One source says the name comes from Jamaica where the crushed flowers are used to polish black shoes. Most likely Papa would not have known, and probably would not have approved this use for his favorite flower. And he possibly would not have been aware that in the arcane Victorian language of flowers hibiscus conveyed the message of change and delicate beauty.

But Papa did know the spectacular flowers the beautiful hedge hibiscus can make, and he took great pleasure in passing by, admiring the abundant stands of the hibiscus hedge where he lived. And it pleased him that hibiscus was always in bloom on Father's Day.

Salute to a Volunteer: Clammyweed

Idle days of winter bring to mind memories of happy botanical accidents, the kinds that offer those curious surges of contentment. This particular "accident" involved a mistaken identity.

It started with a young plant appearing at the very front of a newly prepared bed. Other nursery stock placed there had been selected with much care and the emergence of this rogue, ankle-high planting caused a stir of curiosity. Was it a weed? An interesting variety of tomato perhaps? A hybrid oddity? After some discussion, consensus favored leaving it in place to see what might become of it.

By midsummer a vigorous plant had bolted to four feet high,

branching in all directions of the compass and just as wide. Small, rounded leaves ran the length of the stems, giving the appearance of green fish scales. Each stem terminated in a large, white flower cluster with conspicuous purplish stamens of varying lengths making, on the whole, a most striking garden specimen.

But what especially pleased and delighted all who saw the plant was the way it attracted the butterflies and other insects. It was not uncommon to see several species of butterflies, with as many bees or wasps, hovering about the bush at one time. Visitors commented on its beauty and often paused to watch the numerous insects tending the exotic blooms.

Inquiries failed to identify this botanical showstopper until someone guessed it could be cleome, the so-called spider flower (*Cleome spinosa*).

Yet a nagging doubt persisted based on observations of a few of our mystery plant's distinctive characteristics: a strong musky smell, its sticky feel, and erect seed pods with thin wispy hairs like unplucked eyebrows.

In a continuing search to confirm the plant's identity, a wildflower book set the matter straight. It was clear that our "cleome" was in fact none other than clammyweed (*Polanisia uniglandulosa*).

How would we now face cleome's many admirers? "Clammyweed?" they asked, with special emphasis on *clammy*. Yet disappointment and initial resistance to this unappealing new identity gave way to heartfelt regret when clammyweed met its demise after a windstorm blew it to the ground.

We gathered the remains and broadcast the seed wherever we thought it might flourish: on the hillside, in the gardens, on the parkway in the earnest hope that it would return the following season as a most welcome garden addition.

Zinnias

In the language of flowers zinnias signify "thoughts of absent friends." How appropriate it seems then that seeds for the zinnias we grow at our Brazos House garden first came to us from a dear friend living in Georgia. Each year, high summer brings with it such strong, vivid zinnias, a reminder of that thoughtful person so far away.

As members of the massive Compositae family, zinnias warm the eye as well as the heart. They are not demure or retiring, but are self-proclaiming, blooming in a galaxy of brilliant colors: lemon yellow, red, orange, white, purple, and lilac, all but blue. Their slender petals radiate from the center much like daisies or dahlias; some even look like pom-poms. Planted informally or formally, their plural blooms suggest simplicity and lack of pretense—like good friendships.

Zinnias were cultivated by the Aztecs for centuries before making their way to Europe from their native Mexico in the 18th century. The Spaniards in Mexico must have considered them garish because they dubbed zinnias *mal de ojos*, "bad for the eyes." As a result, the flower remained unappreciated for almost three hundred years until it began to be widely cultivated and "improved" in the 19th century.

It was Swedish botanist, physician, and zoologist Carl Linnaeus (1707-78) who first applied the name "zinnia" to these delightful flowers. He named them for Johann Gottfried Zinn a 16th century professor of medicine at Göttingen University in Germany who wrote about the anatomy of the human eye. "Zinn's zonule" was named for him as well, a medical term used to describe a set of radiating fibers along the lens of the eye. It was perhaps this image of multiple rays, brought to light by Zinn's treatise, which inspired Linnaeus's name for the flowers.

Zinnias range in height from about six inches for dwarfs, to three feet for tall varieties. *Zinnia elegans,* or common zinnias, are the most popular. As sun-loving annuals which are both heat and drought resistant, they are worthy denizens of the South and Southwest. There is also the narrow leaf zinnia (*Z. linearis*), which forms a compact mound of small, saffron-colored flowers about a foot tall. This was the zinnia of the Aztecs, and it too, tolerates hot, dry conditions. Dwarf varieties make excellent edging, rockery or container plants, while the taller varieties are useful in beds and back borders.

Simple to cultivate, zinnias are an ideal choice for novice gardeners or for children to try. They may be sown in pots, broadcast over bare soil, or allowed to self-sow. We let ours reseed, and year after year they come back to dazzle with bright blooms from summer until frost. Grow in a rich, well-drained soil, in full sun, and with good air circulation. Resow every two weeks for continuous flowering throughout the season.

Although zinnias require little care, they look best if given a good top dressing of compost about midsummer, along with a deep soaking. Deadhead regularly if brown, spent blossoms bother you. In areas of high winds, staking may be necessary for taller varieties.

Amiable though they are, zinnias benefit from thinning to help avoid powdery mildew. A more dispassionate gardener might find thinning an enjoyable task, but for me it is difficult to remove even a single one of those bright disks from its stem. Instead, I "thin" by cutting to bring indoors. Zinnias make a pert addition to any flower arrangement with vase life lasting often five to seven days.

Hosts of nectar gatherers are attracted to zinnias; it is not uncommon to find a dozen or more bees, and eight to ten butterflies flickering in our small plot.

Years ago there was a house in Dallas with a long, broad parkway planted in zinnias. By July it was ablaze in glorious color. A handmade sign on a wooden stake driven into the ground at a rakish angle read: "Please Pick the Zinnias." Only once did I spot someone actually gathering them.

Offering those zinnias to passersby always struck me as an exceptional act of goodwill.

Chapter 3
Garden(ing) Retrospections

Thoughts on a Garden in January

Many gardeners consider January the bleakest month, brightened only by the avalanche of flower and seed catalogs overtaking their mailboxes. Although some may admit to enjoying a hearty stew by fireside on a cold winter's evening, or seem grateful for an occasion to wear grandmother's hand-knit sweater, still they yearn for warm-season fruits, and the comfortable temperatures of spring and early summer when the sweater can be set aside in favor of a well-worn tee shirt purchased at the farmer's market. Some may assert that January days are too short, and the nights too long; too much time is spent indoors, it being too cold to sow seeds, too dark to see what must be done in the garden.

No doubt January has its dreary aspects, but also it brings opportunity for a productive survey of one's garden. January's stark, crisp light allows for a clear look, and stamping about the frozen ground, I resolve this year to really *observe* the garden. Without the distraction of riotous color supplied by blooming plants of the warmer months, the garden appears barren, revealing all the flaws of its structure and design. Neglected tasks from months before emerge like specters to menace the spirit: over there are the many unrestrained rose branches, too brittle now from the cold to tether without breaking; the irises are awaiting division; that section of fence where the wisteria bullied its way through the iron panels needs repair; shrubs that should have been moved to better locations years ago, or pansies that might have been planted in the courtyard for a little winter cheer, all need attention. Discouraged, I am near to believing that the garden will never amount to more than an awkward collection of misplaced plants warped and scarred by freeze and neglect.

Ready to end this day's rather grim review and return indoors, my eyes settle upon the compost heap. Staring at that stockpile of dried, discarded, decaying remnants brings to mind Walt Whitman's words from "This Compost," in *Leaves of Grass* : earth "grows such sweet things out of such corruptions . . . it gives such divine materials to men, and accepts such leavings from them at the last." Somewhat heartened by these thoughts of transformation and regeneration, I begin to examine the garden anew. What seemed so barren at first inspection now appears merely dormant, resting in that period when plants await earth's mysterious signal to begin their transition to another season.

But the flaws and neglected tasks discovered earlier point to a larger fault: overemphasis on the garden's visual appeal at the expense of other elements. A garden is, after all, more than a sum of many little plants exploding with color in all the right, weed-free places. It must have structure, formed by borders, shrubs, or walkways; it must have a soul, felt in the peace one finds there, and its character shaped by the circumstances of geography.

Equally important, the dimension of time in a garden, as represented by the seasons, makes the month of January all the more enigmatic. Positioned at the head of a new calendar year, January is named for the Roman god Janus, god of beginnings, guardian of doors and gateways. Representations of Janus usually depict him as having two heads: one looking back and the other looking forward, an attribute that seems fitting for presiding over a garden.

Each winter I try taking to heart Whitman's lesson of the compost heap by being more mindful of the garden's restorative energies, and to take a cue from Janus, celebrating all that the garden has been while looking ahead to what it promises to become.

The Seed Box

As each calendar year begins anew gardeners often go in search of their cache of seeds. A rollick through the catalogs may give rise to dreams of that perfect garden, firing the imagination and prompting a rummage through any seeds on hand.

Unfortunately, my seed supply suffers a disordered existence. Its containers vary: old glass canning jars with rusted lids, coffee cans with labels removed, plastic snack bags that won't stay shut, muddy yogurt containers, torn coin envelopes, recycled film canisters and medicine bottles, or seed packets that now must be stored upside down because their flaps were removed in haste by shivering fingers on some earlier January morning.

Treasured seeds deserve better to be sure. And initially mine did get better treatment, organized and arranged in a large cardboard box with compartments made of cardboard dividers, segregated according to a scheme based on planting times.

Although the system is more willy-nilly now, in the seed box heyday each seed packet was stored in a designated section and in alphabetical order within its section. So, for example, behind the divider marked "Cool Season—Half-Hardy; Plant Feb. 19 to Mar. 19 (Start seed indoors no later than Feb. 1)" there appeared the seed packets for beets, broccoli, cabbage, cauliflower, chard, kale, onions, radishes, snap peas, and turnips in that order.

The flower seeds, also alphabetized but without dividers, occupy the longest continuous row within the box. Beginning with amaranth, it's easy to tab through to cleome, four-o'clocks, a fat packet of godetia, multiple envelopes of hollyhocks, moonflowers, morning glories, and poppies, an assortment of sunflowers and sweet peas, and ending with zinnias. Seed given by friends are clearly marked with name and date or location, reviving warm memories of friendship whenever I come across the gift envelope. Each January I select from among all the flower seeds, banding together by seasonal planting times those that will go in the ground for the year's garden.

The section marked "Miscellaneous Collected Seeds" has the most interest and value for me. Here reside several dozen or so of the diverse and disordered packets of seeds collected on travels. While we made stops along roadsides, my patient husband would wait for me while I scribbled on a rumpled envelope some cryptic descriptive information such as "Shrub-like Miniature Mesquite (with pods) from Langtry, Texas. Collected Fall, 1996." Or, "Mystery Vine from Holiday Inn @ Uvalde, Texas. Collected Fall, 1996." At the time, while their appearance was fresh in the mind's eye, there was every intention of looking up the specimens, to fix their identity on our return, but the research was neglected, and now I can't remember many of the plants.

Most likely some of the seeds are dried and useless by now, but I cannot bear to part with them. The jumble of new seed packets mixed in with the old represents a kind of gardening record; some of my efforts were fruitful, others not. The seeds also serve as reminders of nature's secrets, secured so tightly within the perfect packaging of a tiny seed.

If ever my seed box is to be rearranged, it will be after I am gone. My husband has clear instructions on what to do. He has promised to empty the contents of the seed box, mix and blend all the seeds together, then scatter them at one time in our gardens.

Imagine the possibilities. We can only hope that nature—and the seeds—will understand.

A Gardener's Query: Yard or Garden?

During a group trip to visit gardens of the Pacific Northwest, I overheard an acquaintance remark wistfully that *this* (the splendid Vancouver garden on view before us) is a *garden* and that what she has back home is a *yard*. People generally *walk across a yard*, she explained, but *stroll through a garden*. Karen's observations caused a ripple of commentary among the others in the group. A few of them replied with distinctions of their own between yards and gardens.

The episode later prompted an informal poll to explore the subject further. So in the months following the trip, I posed this question to a few friends and family: "What is the difference between a yard and a Garden?" Here is a sampling of my findings:

Ken: "A yard can be any kind of yard: a lumberyard, a brickyard, a train yard, Scotland Yard. . . . You mow the yard, but you tend a garden."

Kim: "A garden is cultivated, it's visually stimulating. People in other cultures, like in Europe for example, use the word 'garden' when talking about what we call a 'yard.' I think of a lawn, by the way, as being bigger than a yard."

Kath: "A yard has grass to cut. Kids play in the yard; it's utilitarian. A garden is a thing of beauty, a place of delight, a place to look forward to spending leisure time. I wouldn't eat from a yard, but I would eat from a garden. A yard is for trolls. A garden is for butterflies and fairies."

Charles: "A yard is a landscaped area around a house or building. A garden is a specific location for specialty planting within a yard. There you can have a flower garden, a vegetable garden, a rock garden, and so on. A garden is visually decorative."

Jenny: "A yard is more grass than plants; it's controlled. A garden has a focus, like flowers. You just sit in a yard, but a garden requires interaction. There's more of a relationship with a garden. A yard is a piece of ground. A garden is lovingly sculpted."

And this from garden writer Martha Smith from her book *Beds I Have Known : Confessions of a Passionate Amateur Gardener*:

> A garden is a combination trading post, encounter group, social center, and workout class. It can be a place of great serenity and calm or the scene of hot debate. With the asking of one innocuous question, a garden can become a fascinating impromptu classroom where lessons are taught about plant science, growing techniques, and the essentials of life itself.

From the *Pocket Oxford Dictionary*: "Yard n. a piece of enclosed ground esp. attached to building(s) or used for a particular purpose. Garden n. piece of ground for growing flowers, fruit, or vegetables . . . grounds laid out for public enjoyment."

Random thoughts of my own: You sod a yard. You plant a garden. A yard contains the present. A garden contains the future. A yard is maintained. A garden sustains. A yard is duty. A garden is beauty.

In asking the difference between yards and gardens, it appears that the consensus favors gardens. Yet no disparagement of yards is intended, for yards are necessary components of the whole. Yards often will lead us to the garden, providing it with a vista, backdrop, or enclosure. The yard can be the setting for the garden jewel contained within. If the yard is the body, the garden is its soul.

What also has emerged in the responses is the spontaneous feeling expressed for gardens. For many people the garden represents more than a mere collection of plants. It is a metaphor for life and its mysteries.

It has been said that "the garden is a plot of new beginnings." Just so. Perhaps it is time to think of our gardens, and yards, in just this way. We can begin afresh, remembering the lessons learned from our yards and gardens, relying on what is real and timeless. We can be more earnest in our partnership with nature. We can try to understand her handiwork more intelligently and to guard her laws more vigilantly. We can renew our commitment to organic principles and techniques.

And if we wish, we can become yardeners as well as gardeners.

Thistle While You Work

For many years we used to spend weekends at the family farm in a nearby county. And every September we looked forward to the purple thistles appearing along the ridge of a large berm that formed the earthen dam of a pond. There in the liquid sunlight of approaching autumn, spreading colonies of thistles glowed in metallic shades of deep violet tinged with sky blue. Such arresting colors combined with the spiny-toothed leaves and slender branching candelabra stems of plants standing rigid, in heights ranging from one to three feet as they reflected iridescent in the water, gave an almost cosmic effect.

The otherworldly beauty of the thistles provided welcome distraction while working at chores within their proximity. Occasionally the thistles induced fanciful imaginings of breaking away from the work long enough to announce this singular sight to anyone around who might listen. But, of course, pride and common sense overcame such a foolish impulse.

Anyway, the folks who might have heard such nonsense likely would have known that those were not *real* purple thistles at all, but *false* purple thistles. In his book *Adventures with a Texas Naturalist* Roy Bedichek has a few words on the subject:

> Mistakes, especially botanical errors, are sometimes corrected in rough-and-ready fashion by the simple application of the word 'false' to the name. For instance, a certain plant is called at first a thistle, but to distinguish it from another thistle, color is added and it's a purple thistle. But the trouble is, a different plant already goes by that name and confusion arises. Then the new claimant to the name is discovered on closer inspection not to be a thistle at all, so it is named a 'false purple thistle.' And so on.

And so it was with our purple thistles which were not thistles at all but were, in fact, known as eryngo, or *Eryngium leavenworthii*. Named for 19th century discoverer Melines Conklin Leavenworth a U. S. Army surgeon, botanist, and explorer, *E. leavenworthii* claims membership in the Umbelliferae family, making it cousins to vegetables such as carrots, celery, and parsnips; and to herbs or spices such as, parsley, dill, fennel, coriander, chervil, and cumin.

Regardless of its real or its false name, or of its pedigree, what we loved best about eryngo was its unusual appearance and striking color. A few stems gathered, dried, and placed in a vase made handsome, decorative arrangements that lasted for weeks on table or mantel.

E. leavenworthii grows mainly on the chalky, limestone soils of plains, prairies, and grasslands. Unfortunately, it does not transplant well, but some sources suggest that if seeds are sown when ripe they may establish in a garden and flower two years later. Too bad we did not know this at the time, for had we collected seed those many years ago we might now be enjoying eryngo on the property we have today.

For now, come every September we think of thistles as we work and content ourselves with the memory of the farm's eryngo glowing in the autumn sun.

The Potting Shed

This year more than ever thoughts of a different way of being seem to occupy the mind. Things will change, we say, now that the cosmic chronometer has rolled over to year 2000. We expect to see all aspects of our lives improved. Our bodies will be sleeker, our relationships more meaningful, our lives and spaces more organized, our finances better regulated, our time put to highest and best use. Our gardening, too, will be infused with a renewed sense of purpose and energy. A "New Order" will prevail.

For me the New Order takes shape in a favored spot, the potting shed. A gift from my husband some seven or eight years ago to mark a special birthday, the potting shed is a timeless place. Here the only clock is the sun's clock—or the moon's, or a bird's—and sunrises blend into sunsets. In this petite space with large, south-facing windows overlooking the glistening lake beyond, the most celebrated birthday is a seed's birth-day. There is a secret urge to cheer the indomitable life force displayed by a tiny seedling as it emerges and pushes up, shoving aside its bit of soil. In the New Order of things it might not be hard to imagine ourselves as that stout little seedling, effortlessly tossing burdensome cares away like loose bits of soil. Around the potting shed the celebrated years are the years of delicious rains in August, or ones of good harvest when we enjoy out-standing sweet potatoes or heirloom okra, or the spectacular fall display of repeat blooming roses. In the New Order, the best years will be remem-bered for the joys they brought; the bad ones for the lessons learned. Within the protective enclosure of the potting shed we might fancy ourselves immune to time, causing us to muse that the year of a new

39

century or a new millennium is, after all, rather more human invention than significant occasion.

From the potting shed the imagination takes wing. With time-lapse speed, we might look past the bare branches of a pecan tree or beyond the containers of spent pansies to see our garden transformed, no matter the season, into a splendid confection of plants. The seasons merge and blend seamlessly, giving forth choice garden varieties which may bloom outside their appointed time. We might see the vitalizing color of poppies in spring partnered with the golden crocuses of autumn. In this imaginary garden setting there may be larkspur and moon vine, daffodils and zinnias; purple clematis artfully arranged over a white cascading rose. Our minds seduced by glossy garden catalogs, the whole picture is, of course, a lovely succession of plants and flowers at the height of their glory, blissfully unaffected by the tedium of weeds and insects. But the New Order demands a more realistic vision; it allows only those plants that grow and prosper where and when they are meant to be.

Tools and accouterments collected earnestly over the years fill the shelves of the potting shed: garden gadgets that never worked, even when new; broken plant labels; dried up permanent marker pens; bent trowels and claw diggers. In the New Order these will be tossed out so that only the best-loved, most-used, and most efficient equipment will occupy space: the yellow kneeling pad, the Japanese hand pick, the green and amber leather gloves, the curved harvest knife, the wooden planting stick from Czechoslovakian friends, the Model 50 secateurs which are *never* lent to anyone.

There are the fragrances, too. The unmistakable freshness of homemade compost: dark, moist, and fluffy, the sacred fuel for everything we grow. Pungent fish emulsion, now just a residual ring of sediment in the bottom of a watering can; a fresh peach, its flesh broken by a hungry bird's beak finds its ripeness on the potting shed bench. This rich redolence is a reminder of life's continuum.

Itself a celebration, the potting shed is a place of peace, harmony, and growth. It is both garden and gardener. It might be said that a garden actually begins in the potting shed. Then afterward, it is just a question of time.

One Gardener's Thanksgiving

As a group, gardeners tend to be a thankful and generous lot. They often find happiness in small things such as receiving a bonus packet of seeds with a purchase from a nursery catalog—especially appreciated when the seeds arrive in time for the current planting season. Gardeners are thankful for information and exchange it freely. They are thankful for rain, for sun, for shade. They are pleased to share plants and thankful for plants given to them, even if there's no room left in the garden to plant them. In these instances the receiver appreciates the impulse of the giver to share a good thing, to pass along a special plant to someone who might give it a good home.

Though memory now sometimes clouds even important things, I am thankful that mine seems intact enough to recall the generous gifts made to us for our gardens. For instance, on learning of our interest in antique roses, our elderly neighbor, Nell, gave us a rose whose mother plant is over one hundred fifty years old; friend Pat rose early one morning to dig and pot up the starts of fresh mint from her garden, then delivered them despite a long drive ahead to care for her ailing husband and elderly, terminally ill mother; clumps of tall ruellia were given in stages by friend Phyllis who remembered our desire to stabilize and cover an eroding hillside; a local old-timer named Doyle gave us dried pods containing heirloom okra seeds, thus launching our first successful experiments with this magical, mysterious vegetable; Clark and Barbara gave us divisions from their enviable stand of purple asters; cuttings of the rose "Veilchenblau" were given to me by my mother in memory of my grandmother; and zinnia seeds sent years ago by my friend Edie from Georgia reseed to this day.

My husband's former business associate, a man named Don, first gave us the "Brazos" blackberry shoots that comprise our existing blackberry patch. Later, after learning that our stand of an unusual variety of raspberries had died, Don shared shoots from the ones we had given to him on an earlier occasion remembering, he said, how important it was to us to keep the gene pool alive. Schoolteacher Lynn, noting my growing curiosity about climbing spinach "Malabar," made a ninety mile round trip drive to deliver several pots of it with a caring message besides. And our writer friend Jeffrey brought thoughtful hospitality gifts of Thai basil and an exotic curry plant.

These represent a small sampling of the many meaningful gifts made to our garden over the years. And the memories of them extend to memories of the givers themselves, thereby populating our garden not only with their plants, but with fond reminiscences of the generous people who cared enough to give them.

The sweet civility of the late autumn months brings to mind these remembrances and inspires gratitude. I am grateful for November: crisp air and crackling fires scented with cedar. I am grateful, indeed, for the many trees my husband has saved and planted, for their fine structure becomes more apparent after dropping their leaves this time of year; I am grateful, too, for his poetic appreciation of the natural world and for the potting shed he had built to mark a new decade in my life. I appreciate the many years of service given by Mike in the form of weekly help on our property, for his care, his horticultural knowledge, and his work ethic.

I am thankful to the individuals who have visited our gardens and to those who took time to articulate or write about how important the experience was for them, how it refreshed their spirit and renewed their sense of wonder for and connection to the natural world.

Perhaps we humans are not the only grateful ones. Does it seem odd to imagine that plants might be grateful, too? Perhaps the nandina and pyracantha berries, so perfectly formed and brilliant at this season, just might be evidence of their own brand of gratitude for being set out to grow in the right place, under right conditions. And the rose hips, grateful to have their moment in the sun now that the rose flowers are gone? Gaggles of geese honk overhead; no doubt they appreciate the food they are about to receive from the caring man across the lake who feeds them.

Gratitude has many guises and, happily, is timeless. For this gardener thanksgiving is not confined to a single designated day. It occurs each and every day—in and around the activities of our gardens here.

Spring Days

JARDIN DES FLEURS

Chapter 4
Seasons in the Garden

Spring Days

When spring's siren song can be heard again, it often beckons gardeners to their patches of growing-ground. Emerging from wintry cocoons, we retune ourselves to the chorus of sights, sounds, fragrances, and energies of the season. Glimpses of purple iris; the tantalizing fluttering of crepe-like poppies; the chatter of gregarious purple martins, now returned to their nesting houses; the perfume of sweet peas and wisteria; or the surge of a spring breeze brushing past the ear combine to make a gardener susceptible to nature's allure.

In spring we drop to our knees to transplant tomatoes out into the soft spring mud, or maybe instead just linger inside the potting shed a moment longer to watch a gentle April rain. Isn't everyone a gardener in springtime? Even those who may part their curtains only for an early morning gaze out their window might now stare, astonished, at the splendor of banks of azaleas, or the massed plantings of swollen tulips. Enchanted by a neighbor's pert primroses, they may hasten to purchase some of their own, or to install on the front porch colorful hanging baskets containing avalanches of begonias.

Some curious internal rumblings cause this restive gardener to rush to the tool shed in search of rake and claw digger. There is much to be done in anticipation of spring's exuberant displays. Spent winter mulch, for instance, must be removed from the base of the rose bushes. Repeated strikes of the claw digger loosen and perforate the soil, allowing it to breathe and more readily accept the season's first amendments. Dressings of compost awaken the nostrils to the damp, earthy smell, and I feel the alchemy of spring beginning to work its magic.

Repetitive motions allow the mind to wander, as I sift through my random thoughts in much the way we screen the rough stuff from our homemade compost. Only the finer material passes through the compost screen; so, too, I'd like to believe, with spring thoughts—only the better ones will remain to hold on to, or to share.

Warming to my tasks, I become aware of that special quality of springtime sunshine, distinctly different from sunshine in the other seasons. The light in spring seems young, soft, and liquid—like early morning light—and seems to stay this way throughout spring days.

Even so, as the light fades at close of day, I feel drawn to reexamine what I've accomplished. Prompted to take one last look at the garden before nightfall, I discover the first tender shoots of asparagus, so easy to miss at dusk on the north side of the vegetable garden. I resolve to watch closely and to harvest them at just the right time.

A male redbird begins to sing to his mate. By some mysterious combination of natural influences he knows when to serenade her, perhaps as encouragement for her approaching stay on the nest. His spirited song accompanies me as I collect the garden tools and prepare reluctantly for return to the house.

The day's experiences combine and orchestrate themselves into pleasant retrospections, bringing to mind author E. B. White's essay "A Report in Spring" and his recollection of a spring day in the country:

> What I most vividly and longingly recall is the sight of my grandson and his little sunburnt sister returning to their kitchen door from an excursion, with trophies of the meadow clutched in their hands—she with a couple of violets, and smiling, he serious and holding dandelions, strangling them in a responsible grip. Children hold spring so tightly in their brown fists—just as grownups, who are less sure of it, hold it in their hearts.

Wisteria Hysteria

And so again I quote E. B. White: "The first day of spring was once the time for taking young virgins into the fields, there in dalliance to set an example in fertility for Nature to follow. Now we just set the clock an hour ahead and change the oil in the crankcase." Speak for yourself, E. B. Some

Wisteria Hysteria

of us do more than set clocks and change the oil in spring. There are some of us who look forward to spring's upheaval. There are some of us who wait for wisteria to bloom.

Wisteria, wisteria, wisteria. Touching one's cheek against those silken, cascading blossoms and inhaling the heady perfume will turn a body's thoughts to love as surely as there were dalliances in those pagan fields of long ago.

Yet like many allurements wisteria has its contradictions. Horticulturist Tom Christopher calls it a "beautiful strangler," for example. The French writer Colette remembered a wisteria from her childhood as a "flourishing, irrepressible despot," charging that it "had a murderous strength" and a "reptilian mind." She watched it and learned "how it covers, strangles, adorns, ruins, and shores up." On the surface these assertions might be construed as bad press. Not so. They are more like the confessions of those who are made powerless by the wisteria's robust embrace.

Each spring my husband and I would willingly succumb to the wisteria's enticements, hopelessly enchanted by the Chinese wisteria entwined about the entry of our then Dallas home where he had planted it many years ago. Its main trunk grew to about eight inches in caliper. It twisted and turned, circled and sprawled, made elegant, muscular volutes in the air reaching and covering the roof. For two glorious weeks in early spring, each time we approached the front door we would pass through a canopy of pendulous amethyst droplets so intoxicatingly fragrant that we became like human bumble bees, buzzing from one blossom to the next.

It was too much to keep to ourselves. So every year or two we celebrated with a Wisteria Festival. Timing was crucial, of course, to capture the moment when the blossoms were at their peak. Seasons of heavy rains or hailstorms will destroy the delicate flowers. In such years our Festival plans were aborted with great regret. So instead of enjoying an after-party glow as intended, we lamented the lavender petals, then ruined and brown, strewing the courtyard. But when the time was right, and Lady Luck spared us storms, we gathered with a few friends to sip champagne as our wonderful wisteria unleashed its scent.

The name sometimes is pronounced wisTARia. An afternoon spent with gardening references revealed why. The plant is named for Caspar Wistar who was a professor of anatomy in the 18th century at the University of Pennsylvania. The English botanist and plant collector Thomas Nuttall thought of as a father of American botany, named the genus in Wistar's honor, but spelled it *Wisteria.*

Wisteria is a member of the pea (Fabaceae) family, which accounts for its fragrance. There are some 10 species of this deciduous, climbing woody vine. The elongated flowers (known as racemes) of *Wisteria* spp. range in color from white to pink, mauve, violet-blue, and deep purple. Chinese wisteria (*W. sinensis*) and Japanese wisteria (*W. floribunda*) are the most commonly seen in our area. Although not as common, there is also American wisteria, sometimes called Texas wisteria (*W. frutescens*).

Japanese wisteria is perhaps the most elegant of all, displaying flowers 24 inches or more in length. Its leafy tendrils lash onto supports in a clockwise fashion. The Chinese wisteria has shorter blooms, but often produces another, though less impressive flush, a couple of months after the spring show. Its stems wind and twist counterclockwise. Both species are vigorous, rampant vines. American or Texas wisteria is less expansive.

Chinese and Japanese wisteria will vault over strong supports in no time. Each offers versatility in the landscape for use as trees, shrubs, or high-climbing vines. Wisteria requires no fertilizer, as fertilization will only produce more leaves and fewer blooms. Deep, well-drained soil is important, as well as discipline by pruning (usually June is the best time) if you wish to keep it within defined bounds. Otherwise it may grow to the topmost limbs of your tallest tree.

Wisteria typically produces blossoms before the leaves—a real bonus for those of us who are impatient for the tints and fragrances of spring. After blooming, Chinese wisteria produces hard, suede-like pods encasing nickel-size seeds the color of dark coffee.

The French novelist and performer Colette remembered the workings of a wisteria as a burglar that at some moment must have shattered the windowpane of a ruined tower she was visiting claiming it "had just struck, broken, and entered." It is no wonder she thought of it in that way, for wisteria can burglarize the heart as well.

The Importance of Being Autumn

The vise-like grip of summertime heat has relaxed into autumn's mellow embrace. At last, no more miserable days will be spent mopping the brow or reshaping the wilted brim of a sun hat. All the mistakes showing up in the gardens by end of summer have receded from its harsh glare. Now gardens become livable again, restored to fresh vibrancy.

The cool air seems to energize. A hint of lower temperatures to come occurred earlier than usual this year, in August, when on a sultry evening, a spontaneous breeze arose. Distinct bands of cold air layered between waves of humid and hot lent mystery to this light wind, so unexpected for the season. It gathered speed as it came over the bluff in the darkness of night, wrapping anything in its path. It whirled, lifted up to me, and then was gone. (Shortly afterward the purple martins departed for their annual migration. Was this curious current of air a seasonal message calling them away?)

The breeze carried other complex messages. Something was about to happen it seemed, an unmistakable coolness announcing the promise of autumn. It suggested an aspect of time, posing the garden world somewhere between now and then.

One writer reported that a soldier-sculptor once called autumn "awe-time" upon seeing masses of asters, or Michaelmas daisies as he knew them. No wonder, for plants in blues and rich lavenders flower as much in the fall as those bearing the sunset tones more commonly associated with the season. Consider, for example, the pale blue plumbago, or English, French and Spanish lavender, the deep blue of Texas bluebells (also called prairie gentian), the blue-violet of Mexican petunia, the violet and white Salvia leucantha, or the lovely blue spiderworts and autumn crocuses.

Of course trees are the real lords of autumn, for time is camouflaged within their leaves."In blossom, now the leaves will bloom/ Their time, and take from milder sun/ an unreviving benison," writes poet Robert Penn Warren. Leaves once green and plump from chlorophyll now "bloom" in flaming hues splotched with titian, orange, gold, and crimson before they fade. With displays of such exuberant color they seem to rally much the same way other living things do before dying.

Featherweight leaves fall from the branches of oak trees. Caught swirling in a plume of autumn wind, they move back and forth with courtly flourishes, making their way to the ground. Joining thousands of others, they collect in damp mats beneath the feet, until the stalwart armies of howling leaf blowers disturb their splendid congregation.

A woolen cap soon replaces the bent-brim sun hat now. And the air, crisp and frank, will bear traces of cedar smoke, sweet as any incense. Pairs of mallard ducks pass overhead, flying so low the whoosh of their pinions can be heard.

Yes, a change of season is here. That August breeze left no doubt.

Good Bones

Autumn glory. A shift in the season causes senses to readjust, tuning themselves in to the sights, sounds, and fragrances of late fall. Eyes appraise the crimsons, russets, ambers, and golds of sweet gum, red oak, pistache trees, and chrysanthemums. They follow the wisps of chilled breath against cool, crisp air, watch the spiraling of a falling leaf, or trace the shape of an odd pumpkin. Ears delight in the harmonies of slow autumn rain, the crush of leaves beneath the feet, or the snap of a dried branch cracked across the knee, sized right for a retriever to fetch. The nose is refreshed by the scents of cedar and juniper, and one may be tempted to find the source of a fragrance like that of apples baking in the oven or persimmon pudding. There is the incense of cedar logs burning in an outdoor fireplace.

Autumn, the flip side of spring. The vibrant, riotous colors of spring have given way to mature, deeper shades of fall. Spring is expansion, fall is contraction. Rest, quiet, and dormancy juxtapose the frenzied growth of spring. Nature seems to be tucking herself in for a spell.

The eye no longer distracted by field poppies or the blossoming rose now sees something else emerge: something of the structure of things. As the mantle of leaves and flowers recedes, the garden reveals what writers sometimes call "the bones of the place." A beloved pecan tree, for example, once layered with leaves and catkins, shows itself in relief, bare branches glistening in early morning frost. And without its leaves, the cedar elm stands now in splendid isolation, displaying its bones with the large arching limb framing a favored view beyond the wooden bench.

As the "bones" of the garden become more apparent in late fall, we have a view beneath the surface into the framework. And skeletal tree branches penciled against the sky are a reflection of the complex network of roots below. The stark contrasts are an opportunity to assess strengths and weaknesses.

American poet and physician William Carlos Williams observing the perfections and imperfections of some damaged leaves writes, "And the eaten leaves are lace." Displayed on my desk is an oak leaf found in a condition just as Williams described. Ravaged by insects, all that remains are the leaf veins, forming a mesh of the finest lace.

Carefully preserved for many years now, the leaf serves as a reminder of the importance of structure. Though tested by time and events, its

Good
Bones

"bones" are intact.

In a way the leaf has become a metaphor for my garden. Despite several years of summer drought, imperfect care and a few losses, the garden remains strong at the core.

Yes, the garden has good bones. And good bones are everything.

February Tasks

The ancient Romans may take credit for naming the month of February. According to *The Old Farmer's Almanac,* the word derives from the Latin *februa,* meaning "to cleanse." For the Romans, Februalia was "a month of purification and atonement," a time to get clean.

This seems a good idea. Some of us may need to clean and straighten up after the holiday activities and from the previous year's accumulations in the garden. By February our own gardens appear to be suffering from lack of attention, though much of this is seasonal doldrums. February is our time to clean, amend and, generally, to plan and restore.

For many North Central Texas gardeners February is pre-spring, when the gray days of winter clear for about a week, bringing temperatures mild enough for working out of doors. Our first bulbs will have emerged— snowdrops, or spring crocuses. Winter-flowering shrubs such as winter-bush honeysuckle sweeten the crisp air with its subtle scent; golden yellow witch hazel, and the rich coral flowers of quince brighten the early year's landscape.

February's work consists of clearing, pruning, shredding, planting, or transplanting. But in some years we may have pre-tasks to complete since we might have neglected to do the annual cleaning and oiling of tools, and to put some order in the potting and equipment sheds as we should have done in January.

Thus, when our first fine February day arrives—possibly ushered in by a spectacular winter sunrise—we will be ready and eager to tackle those jobs set aside for the month. First order of business is removal of fallen leaves in the planting beds. By the time February temperatures begin to rise, the plants beneath the leaves can use a bit of fresh air and sunshine. Except for the most cold-sensitive plants, most of the heavy leaf cover is gathered for later shredding and then added to the compost tumbler.

One of the more important tasks in our garden occurs the third week in February. It is marked on the calendar each year: the pruning of all the antique roses that need trimming to maintain their shape. We also work with any other shrubs or small trees that might require similar attention. (Heavy pruning, as might be required of major trees, for example, is done in January.) All the larger debris is hauled off to the city grinding and mulching place where it is shredded and then given away as coarse mulch to anyone who wants a load.

When the heavy work is complete we can focus energies on planting and transplanting which sometimes calls for a bit of rearranging or re-designing selected areas.

By the time these tasks are done a week is often gone. Returning to the warm indoors and to the *Almanac*, we reread some of the weather lore for tips on forecasting the weather in February:

    —If bees get out in February, the next day will be windy and rainy.

    —Fogs in February mean frosts in May.

    —Winter's back breaks about the middle of February.

But our favorite is:

    —There is always one fine week in February.

Chapter 5
Plant Nature and Nurture

What's a Gardener to *do* in January? Sweet Peas

Like many gardeners, the blizzard of garden catalogs free-falling into the mailbox at the beginning of each year fast-forwards my imagination to thoughts of spring. A few favorite flowers rise up to bloom brilliantly in my imaginary garden setting: roses of course, and poppies, larkspur, morning glories, wildflowers, and then there is the fragrance of sweet peas. "Oh, when the blossoms break . . . like heavenly winged angels, and their pure, cool perfume fills the air, what joy is mine," says Celia Thaxter about sweet peas in her book *An Island Garden*.

Shortly after Celia was writing and gardening on the Isles of Shoals off the coasts of Maine and New Hampshire in the late 19th century, there were close to 300 varieties of sweet peas listed in catalogs. But sadly, owing to a number of factors, only eight of these old varieties remained when the English seedsman Peter Grayson began rescuing them in more recent times. Today, thanks to his worldwide searches, there are about 35 antique varieties available.

Sweet peas (*Lathyrus odoratus*) are natives of Crete, Italy, and Sicily. They were first recorded in 1695 as a Sicilian wildflower by an amateur botanist and monk from Palermo, Father Franciscus Cupani. Four years later Father Cupani sent seeds to an English plant collector. Interest in sweet peas spread, and by 1722 they were being recommended for their exquisite perfume, which has been described as a blend of honey with orange flower.

In the 1870s sweet peas began to be cultivated and hybridized intensively in England, stimulated in part by the great demand for them in the United States. By the turn of the century, breeders had introduced many new varieties including the large-petaled, waved and ruffled varieties which are now the standard in sweet peas.

Common names for sweet peas are lady pea and painted lady pea. They are sun-loving annuals, climbing to heights of 5 to 6 feet by means of tendrils which look like little coils emerging from the ends of leaf stalks. Dainty, fragrant flowers appear in early spring in a broad range of vivid colors: rose, purple, scarlet, mauve, blue, white, cream, even bicolored flowers. There are dwarf varieties as well, only a foot tall.

Often remembered as "the flowers my grandmother grew," sweet peas have filled the winter dreams of generations of gardeners. Their intense fragrance, delicate flowers, and pleasing habit of twining on fences or garden wigwams are reminiscent of cottage-style gardening. As cut flowers they make into glorious bouquets, their scent filling entire rooms. Celia Thaxter proudly displayed her carmine sweet peas "in a red Bohemian glass vase . . . an altar of flowers."

The sweet pea grows quickly in loose, moist, fertile, well-drained soil in zones 3 to 10. Preferring cool temperatures, they are a flower Texas gardeners can plant in fall or winter. I enjoy starting mine in pots in December or January by first soaking the seeds overnight. Emergence then occurs usually within about two weeks. After allowing the seedlings to harden off, I transplant them outdoors in mid to late January in double rows staggered on both sides of a cedar fence fitted with chicken wire to support the stems. In the foreground are planted larkspurs and poppies, all together giving a breathtaking spring display lasting many weeks until the hot weather arrives.

The classsic planting method is to sow seeds in well-dug trenches backfilled with a mixture of loam, manure or compost, and about 20% sand. Add bone meal or wood ashes according to soil type. Plant seeds about two inches deep (they need darkness to germinate). An alternative method is to plant pre-soaked seeds one-half inch deep in sand. This reportedly allows seeds to germinate more quickly. Once in flower, pick spent blossoms frequently to encourage more blooms.

Sweet peas have few problems, although birds—especially sparrows —seem to relish emerging seedlings. At end of season plants may begin to look gangly as their foliage withers in warm weather requiring the stems to be untangled from their supports. Thrips and aphids are sometimes seen, and white mold is occasionally caused by excessive dampness. But I do not remember having to treat sweet peas for much of anything. Maybe this is because they are picked so frequently for sweet-smelling indoor bouquets.

Next time the weather has you at a loss for what to do in the garden in January—or if you simply wish to honor your grandmother—remember sweet peas.

No doubt Celia would approve.

Paradise in a Flower: Bird of Paradise

Gardener's occasionally may encounter certain plants seeming to require a proper introduction before becoming "familiar." This occurred at our Brazos House garden many years ago when my husband and I first spotted a slender, five-foot, multi-stemmed shrub growing beneath a large live oak tree. The shrub was out of bloom at the time, and we puzzled over its leaves for clues to its identity; they reminded us more of a small mimosa or an acacia of some kind. An elderly neighbor came to the rescue, introducing us at last to the bird of paradise (*Caesalpinia gilliesii*) sometimes also call poinciana.

Since that first meeting our bird of paradise has surprised us in several delightful ways. The initial surprise was its flower, of course. Not to be confused with the South African species of bird of paradise (*Strelizia*) often sold in florist shops as showy cut flowers, *C. gilliesii* offers its own version of drama. The blossoms look like tropical birds scattered atop graceful, finely-divided, grey-green foliage. The butter yellow petals of the flowers form a rounded shape, like a songbird's swollen breast. These exotic blooms bear six-inch long, extruded, scarlet-red stamens, reminiscent of the flamboyant tail feathers of a bird in courtship. The marked contrast in color makes a stunning display usually lasting well into fall.

A second surprise was the bird of paradise's tolerance to extreme heat and its ease of cultivation. *C. gilliesii*, have come through relentless sizzling temperatures with little extra care and continued blooming. Rated for USDA Zone 7, it can survive winter lows to 10 degrees Fahrenheit, although ours have survived temperatures lower than that (another surprise). Tolerant of alkaline conditions, it occurs naturally on dry, rocky or sandy soils, and is found in the Gulf States and areas along the Mexican border.

Perhaps the most commonly seen variety is *C. pulcherrima*. Known

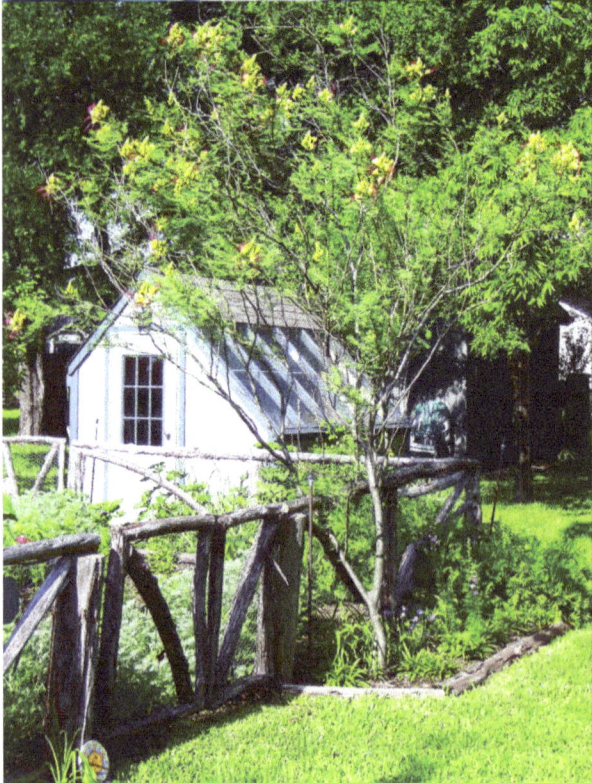

Paradise
in a
Flower

by common names such as red bird of paradise, Barbados flower fence, and Barbados pride, it grows six to eight feet and bears flowers with bright orange petals and dark orange-red stamens. Often used as roadside plantings in the Deep South (Zone 9), its flowers glow in a spectacular blaze of color.

As members of the pea family (Leguminosae, or sometimes attributed to Fabaceae) bird of paradise is easy to grow, making it a good choice for novice gardeners to try. They may be propagated from seed of by softwood cuttings. My preferred method is to start indoors with seed presoaked in warm water overnight, although even this step can be skipped if you are in a hurry or forget. Germination usually occurs within a couple of weeks at about 45-50 degrees Fahrenheit when using a well-drained loam mix. Starts grow quickly, most often remaining pest free.

When ready to plant out, choose a location with full sun. (Our experience demonstrates that yellow bird of paradise will tolerate a little shade, although it will not bloom as profusely as those planted in full sun.) Anticipate staking the slender stems against bullying winds for the first year or two. If you are cramped for space outdoors, bird of paradise is a good candidate for pot culture as well, but be sure to keep it in full sun indoors, too. Only moderate watering is needed—indoors or out—while it matures.

Yellow bird of paradise is a rapid grower, usually making a 4 to 6 six-foot shrub. But in ideal conditions it can reach 10-foot heights. It drops its leaves in winter and rarely needs pruning unless you wish to eliminate a worrisome branchlet or if it freezes back. In that event, pruning it to about 12" to 18" stobs will cause it to resprout and bloom the following summer. Use it in the landscape to form a shrub border or as a specimen plant in a patio or near a pool for a light, airy look. Bird of paradise does not mind other perennials planted at its base to camouflage typically bare stems, if these bother you. Personally, I enjoy its lithe appearance contrasted with denser companions.

The genus *Caesalpinia* was named for Andrea Cesalpino a 16th century Italian botanist and a physician to Pope Clement VIII. The species name, *gilliesii,* comes from the Scottish physician and botanist John Gillies who collected plants in South America. Many of the more than 70 species of *Caesalpinias* are native to tropical areas and are valued for the tannins and dyes they produce.

Now for the last surprise: bird of paradise seeds pop. As the seed pods dry and curl into attenuated ringlets, they eject large, polished, mahogany-colored seeds, the seeds sometimes discharging in many directions at once. Hearing this for the first time, it is easy to mistake those snapping sounds for little cap pistols. Thus, it should come as no surprise that the bird of paradise sports another common name, pop-bean bush.

Autumn is for Amaranth

Summer's staggering temperatures can cause even chiggers to retreat and a few hackberry trees to shed leaves before their time. "And these are the days when whatever you sit down on you stick to," says Ogden Nash in his poem "September is Summer, Too or, It's Never Too Late to be Uncomfortable." If scientific forecasts for worldwide climatic changes prove accurate, we may be obliged to select plants more for their tolerance to heat and drought than for their other merits.

A striking example of heat tolerance in our Brazos House garden is burgundy amaranth (*Amaranthus hypochondriacus*). Amaranth blends resistance to insects, diseases, and adverse weather conditions with the ornamental composure of a fine specimen plant. Bonuses are its nutritional and historical significance.

Burgundy amaranth grows 6 to 8 feet tall. It produces large, crimson seed heads of thick, chenille-like plumes. The exotic spiked seed heads— some measuring the length of elbow to fingertip—rise above leaves splashed with green and purple, reminiscent of coleus in size and coloration. The stalks are usually straight and sturdy, with vertical ribbing like bicolored corduroy.

Burgundy amaranth is an annual vegetable broadleaf plant in the Amaranthaceae family; some 60 species make up the genus *Amaranthus*. Its name is derived from the Greek, *amarantos*, which means unfading or unwithering and likely refers to some of the long-lasting inflorescences.

Better known glamorous cousins in the family include globe amaranth (*Gomphrena*), cockscomb (*Celosia*), and love-lies-bleeding (*A. caudatus*). Its poorer, weedy relatives include pigweed and a variety of tumbleweed.

Our burgundy amaranth usually grows in a north-south row behind trellised tomatoes, making a breathtaking background for the garden. With its majestic plumes erect against a blue sky it looks for all the world like an elite guard standing at attention. Occasionally high winds or exuberant sprinkling can cause a few stalks to topple from sheer weight of their plumage. More often they lean on one another for support, suggesting certain camaraderie. Sometimes we stake them, but prefer to let these handsome sentinels stand unassisted.

Amaranth is easily cultivated in full sun without the use of chemical fertilizers or pesticides. We have experimented with it for many years. While in some seasons it suffered mild attacks of flea beetles or white blister, it has never failed us. It is adaptable to most soil conditions. Start from seed in pots indoors in the spring or direct-seed outdoors after danger of frost. Direct-seeding is usually more effective; transplanting yields mixed results. Sow seeds 1/4" to 1/2" deep. Although seed packets will advise otherwise, we sow seeds thickly, then thin the plants to stand about 8" to 10" apart. This way the mature plants will tend to support one another. If the seed bed is kept moist, emergence can occur in less than one week. As soon as leaves form you will see burgundy amaranth's vivid markings, magenta and green. It will begin producing its distinctive florid plumes in about eight weeks, attaining its full height and grandeur by mid to late summer. By fall (frost or earlier) the seed heads are ready to harvest when they begin to pale.

Harvesting is simple and fun. Cut the tops from the stalks and allow to dry for about a week. We usually place entire seed heads in grocery sacks with a little stalk exposed and tie whole packages upside down to dry in an outbuilding. Drying in this manner allows the tiny seeds (buff-colored and about the size of a poppy seed) to fall into the bottom of the bag, making collection easier. To glean remaining seed after seed heads are fully dry, rub over a standard window screen. This separates seeds from the wooly chaff. Winnowing can be done using a sieve.

The grain produced from the seed is a nutritious food, valued for its protein content. Amaranth supplies lysine, an essential amino acid often missing in grain crops. It is also high in calcium and fiber. Although *A. hypochondriacus* produces what is considered a grain, it differs from most true grains or cereal crops such as corn, which are grasses.

The seeds may be ground—a coffee mill or food processor will do—and the resulting flour added to baked goods boosts protein content. A good proportion is about 25% amaranth flour to 75% wheat or other grain flour. Or the seeds can be cooked into an interesting cereal side dish, much like grits, mixed with other grains and with your choice of flavor enhancers such as garlic, onion, and tomatoes added. Cooked alone (2 cups water to

1 cup amaranth seed; simmer for about 30 minutes) amaranth has a nutty flavor, but has a somewhat gelatinous texture which some people may not like; it resembles "blond caviar." You can also pop the seeds. Popped amaranth is useful as a breakfast cereal, as breading meal, or as a crunchy topping for desserts.

The leaves of burgundy amaranth are edible, too. Used just as you would spinach or turnip greens, they supply Vitamin A, B_6, C, calcium, iron, magnesium, and potassium. The young leaves are best. They have a slightly sweet flavor and are said to have optimal iron content in the seventh week of growth. The mature leaves are edible as well, but tend to be fibrous. The flavor at this stage resembles a mild kale. Although leaves of burgundy amaranth are flavorful, a better choice for simple greens might be one of the many leaf varieties of amaranth, such as merah (*A. gangeticus*). We have not yet cultivated merah, but it is reported to be a beautiful, heat tolerant green, a good replacement for spinach when Texas weather becomes too hot to grow spinach.

In addition to its ornamental and nutritional value, amaranth has historical significance. Archeological evidence from the Tehuacan Valley of Mexico suggests grain amaranth was an ancient foodstuff in use as early as 7,000-5,000 B. C. Much later it became important to the Aztecs who grew it as a sacred crop and used it as a dietary staple and for paying tribute to their emperor Montezuma. They would form a paste of amaranth, honey and other ingredients to make images of their god, Huitzilopochtli. In the early 16th century, the Spanish conqueror of the Aztecs, Hernán Cortés, ordered destruction of the amaranth fields, prohibiting its cultivation and use in religious ceremonies; infractions were punishable by death. It soon disappeared as a major food source and knowledge of it was eclipsed for centuries. But amaranth quietly survived suppression because of its nutritional value and its ease of cultivation with simple hand tools.

Amaranth, like maize, was transported along ancient trade routes, appearing as far north as the Colorado Plateau where seed-gathering Indians of the area used wild and cultivated varieties of amaranth. Evidence of it has been found as far east as the Ozarks. Today *Amaranthus* species continue to be cultivated in remote parts of Central and South America, and in the Sierra Madre region of Mexico where the Tarahumara Indians use amaranth in tamales and tortillas. It is also cultivated in Africa, China, and Nepal.

Apart from amaranth's ornamental and historical significance, it is

Amaranth

63

potentially one of the most important "miracle" crops of the next century, especially for the developing world. Its hardiness, exceptional nutritional content, and ease of cultivation provide the basis for interest in scientific research to develop amaranth for large-scale cultivation in the wheat-growing regions of the U. S.

A final note: a large garden plot is not necessary to grow burgundy amaranth. Just two or three plants are sufficient to make a showy display and produce a modest supply of seed. Birds love amaranth, sometimes causing a succession crop to emerge from fallen seed. But these new plants are easily plucked out if you find them undesirable in your garden scheme.

Consider cultivating amaranth; you will be rewarded with a useful, easy to grow, healthy plant. And when you experience its stunning crimson seed heads, perhaps you won't mind that September is summer, too. Burgundy amaranth's color surely will evoke autumn for you.

The Venerable Pomegranate

Late autumn usually brings pomegranates to market for use in festive dishes or to enhance floral arrangements on holiday tables. Although prized in many Mediterranean countries and parts of Asia, pomegranates are sometimes overlooked in this country by cooks and gardeners alike.

Consider the pomegranate's ancient history. Its cultivation has been important since early times. There are numerous references to pome-granates in the Old Testament. Moses, for example, cites them as one of the desirable foods of the Promised Land. The ancient Hebrews adorned their priestly vestments with embroidered pomegranates. Images of pomegranates were carved on the pillars of Solomon's temple, and he praised his Shulamite bride with allusions to them. Some historians suggest King Solomon's crown was inspired by the pomegranate's upright calyx, providing the basis for the subsequent design of crowns through the ages.

The Egyptians, Greeks, and Romans valued pomegranates for their multiple culinary and medicinal qualities. Greek philosopher Theo-phrastus, generally credited with founding the science of botany, recorded his observations about pomegranates around 300 B. C. And in the 1st century A. D. Pliny the Elder, the Roman naturalist, considered pome-granates among the most useful of ornamental and medicinal plants. Greeks and Romans regarded the pomegranate so highly they devised complex mythologies about it, endowing this enticing fruit with legends rich in symbolism.

Because of its multitude of seeds, pomegranates have been an age-old symbol of fertility. In classical Greek mythology, the pomegranate was the attribute of the beautiful Persephone, daughter of Demeter, the goddess of agriculture and fertility. When Hades, god of the underworld, abducted and ravished Persephone, her mother searched the world for her missing daughter. In grief and desperation Demeter refused to bless the harvests, afflicting the earth with famine, pestilence, and sterility. Through vigorous intervention and negotiation by the god Zeus, Persephone was restored to her mother. But because the girl had eaten six pomegranate seeds secretly forced on her by Hades, she was allowed to spend only half the year with her mother. The other six months she spent in the under-world with Hades, one month for each seed she had consumed. Thus for the ancients, fall and winter occurred when Persephone was separated from her mother; spring and summer accompanied her return to earth. From this myth the pomegranate derives its secondary symbolism of immortality and resurrection.

From Pliny's time pomegranates were known to the Romans as "apples from Carthage." Later, their botanical name became *Pomum granatum*, "apple (or fruit) full of grains." Eventually, pomegranates acquired their current genus and species name *Punica granatum*, "grains from Carthage." Modern poet Ogden Nash offers another explanation in his poem "The Pomegranate":

> The hardest fruit upon this planet
> Is easily the ripe pomegranate.
> I'm halfway through the puzzle game
> Of guessing how it got its name.
> The pome part turns my cowlick hoary,
> But the granite is self-explanatory.

Pomegranates are thought to have originated in Persia (Iran) and Afghanistan. Handsome ornamentals, they make excellent hedges, espaliers, and container plants. Typically they are multi-stemmed bushes reaching heights of 10 to 15 feet, sometimes taller. They can be pruned to a single trunk, forming a small tree. Dwarf varieties also are available.

Pomegranates are easily cultivated in full sun and are not fussy about soil as long as there is sufficient drainage. They grow best in hot, dry climates. This makes the pomegranate a good fruit choice for most of Texas.

65

Mature, they withstand drought well and are long-lived, but do not tolerate low temperatures for long periods. Generally they are trouble free.

Pomegranates are grown mostly for their globular fruits and are about the size of a large orange. The rind is smooth, thick, and leathery, turning from yellowish-red to light red when ripe. Clusters of small, juicy, crimson seeds are embedded in a white pulp. As the fruits enlarge and begin to color, the branches arch gracefully from weight of the ripening fruit, looking much like randomly placed Christmas ornaments. The ruffled flowers are striking. They range in colors from rich vermillion to white, pink, or variegated.

If you enjoy preparing foods pleasing to the eye as well as to the palate, pomegranates offer an exceptional garnish for just about anything. A few seeds enliven a ho-hum salad; the juice makes a cooling drink, or an unusual marinade for meat or poultry. A simple dessert of ice cream or tapioca becomes tantalizingly exotic and elegant with a light sprinkling of the ruby-red seeds which are an excellent source of fiber and are low in fat and sodium. They also contain vitamin C and potassium. If its beauty and nutritional value are not persuasion enough, consider the prophet Mohammed's injunction: "Eat the pomegranate, for it purges the system of envy and hatred."

Preparing pomegranates for the table takes a little patience, but is worth the effort. Wear an apron as juice from the seeds can splatter and stain. Slice the fruit in half, break the seed chambers into workable sections, separate seeds from the surrounding membrane, then store them in a container in the refrigerator where they will be ready for use as needed. I prepare the whole fruit at one time.

Pomegranates can be dried for decorative use. Hang entire branches with fruits attached to air-dry. People who have had success with this method caution that fruits can take up to several months to dry, and they can rot in the process. They advise using small fruits.

Other uses for pomegranates include dyes for carpets. The Moors used the rinds to tan leather. Medical applications, which are a part of pomegranate lore, include nostrums for treatment of dysentery and tapeworm.

Next time at the supermarket, tarry a while at the pomegranate bin. Do not pass them by. Or better yet, cultivate your own for food, for enjoyment, and to be reminded of the pomegranate's rich and ancient history.

Chapter 6
Garden Books

Dear Mr. Jefferson

There is a book I recommend to every serious gardener and history buff. Laura Simon's book *Dear Mr. Jefferson: Letters from a Nantucket Gardener* is fresh, engaging, instructive, witty, and wise.

Laura Simon lives year round on Nantucket Island and has gardened there since 1973. A writer of historical romances by profession, she is a gardener by passion. In her introduction to *Dear Mr. Jefferson*, she relates the logical progression of events and ideas leading to the writing of a series of imaginary letters to that other passionate gardener, Thomas Jefferson. She admits that "it's a bit of a conceit, this business of writing letters to Thomas Jefferson," but that she was seeking a way to communicate "the gardening thrall" which had suddenly overtaken her. With a gardening calendar and clipboard overflowing with comments, observations and lists, she has an intense need to express herself. She has an urge "to discuss soil tilth and tillage, to compare varieties of carrots . . . to brag about getting rosemary seeds to sprout. . . ." In short, she "wanted to talk shop."

Talk shop she does. In a warm and breezy style—as though corresponding with a close friend—she tells Mr. Jefferson about how her collection of vegetables, flowers, and fruit trees evolved from "a tangle of zucchini and brambles" into a kitchen *garden*. The emphasis here is hers, for she feels the elation of self-sufficiency and the celebration of life, these gifts coming from a garden which sustains her and her husband. Simon tells Jefferson about gardening by the seasons, about pampering her onions, putting up stores of canned goods for the cold months, and converting the guest room into a nursery for sprouting seeds.

She brings him up to date on events in gardening history over the last few centuries, deploring the widespread use of chemicals in the twentieth century and the damage they have caused. She imagines how shocked he would be to see a nation, once primarily agrarian, now composed of a population relying chiefly on agribusinesses and supermarkets for its food. She gives him a rundown on how and why seed catalogs got started—a fascinating chapter that stands on its own. She is spellbound by the late summer flowering of a *Mirabilis longiflora,* better known as four o'clock, then suggests that seven o'clock might be a more accurate name. "But that's quibbling," she says.

History enthusiasts will appreciate Simon's meticulous research. By using Jefferson's letters, garden diaries, and maps of plantings at his beloved Monticello, Jefferson the gardener emerges alongside Jefferson the statesman, inventor, architect, and family man. Ever mindful of the great offices he held during his lifetime, she signs off each letter with "Please accept the assurance of my great esteem and respect." This "is a phrase I borrowed from him," Simon says, "a phrase whose eighteenth-century civility remains unmatched today."

Despite such formality and the separation of centuries, it is easy to picture Simon and Jefferson strolling together on the grounds at Monticello. There among the snapdragons, African marigolds, and cleomes, I imagine them conversing in that intense way gardeners enjoy when exchanging information. He, with a polite ear cocked to hear a gardener's tale, and she, gesturing and talking with ebullient wonder and delight.

Politics and the span of time do divide, but gardens bring people together in magical ways. For me now, after reading this book, Jefferson and Simon will be linked together always.

Laura Simon's book is a love story about gardens, really, about Jefferson's garden, her garden, gardens in history, and the future of gardens. But it is more than a gardening book; this volume can take its place in the ranks of gardening literature.

Mr. Jefferson, if I may say so, and with the assurance of my great esteem and respect, Laura Simon has done you, and herself, mighty proud.

A Cautionary Tale

This is a cautionary tale intended for the budding rose enthusiast. If you are an intense person with an appreciative eye and a discerning nose, with an open heart and working hands and, with a head susceptible to romantic history, heed this warning: DO NOT begin to study or acquire Old Garden Roses unless you are prepared to dedicate yourself to them.

The seed of my own capitulation took root in 1992 while browsing the shelves of garden books at a local nursery. Engaged at that time in a landscaping project developing gardens at the property my husband and I had acquired a couple of years earlier, I began searching for titles having to do with Texas and Southern gardens. The spine of William Welch's book *Antique Rose for the South* caught my eye, and I began to examine the book's contents, soon finding, for instance, that "The Apothecary Rose" (*Rosa gallica officinalis*) is a rose "of great antiquity" and that "until the importation of the China Roses, 'Autumn Damask' was the only rose in Europe that flowered again after the spring season."

I discovered that there were organized groups of individuals who would search out old roses—"rose rustlers" they call themselves—and I determined to be one. There also were tantalizing tips about arranging old roses, rose crafts, and the like. All of this was new to me and I felt the thrill of a growing enthusiasm take hold.

Not long afterwards I discovered *Landscaping with Antique Roses* by Liz Druitt and Michael Shoup. Here were helpful hints on techniques for the caring of the Old Garden Roses, their propagation and integration into a landscape design. But it was the gallery of rose portraits with their fascinating histories that I found most appealing. Their individual stories and photogenic beauty fired by imagination. My fate was now sealed. The only way to satisfy this new passion was to acquire a few of the Old Garden Roses for myself.

"A few" turned into about a hundred over the course of several years. My husband indulged me by driving great distances so that we might attend some of the rose rustles, visit rose gardens, or go to distant nurseries to purchase the rose that was "just right" for that vacant spot in our garden. He made countless trips up and down stairs lugging heavy boxes of rose books, and underwrote the design and installation of some thirty linear feet of new bookshelves to accommodate my burgeoning garden library.

Moreover, long weekend hours have been spent in the potting shed experimenting with rose propagation, or developing formulas for soil improvement and amendment. I have studied the roses, fretted over borers, fussed about aphids, obsessed over black spot, planted, pruned, learned from, and loved our antique roses. Also, sadly, we have lost a few of the most prized ones.

In better times I have smelled deeply of the full blossoms of "Souvenir de la Malmaison" or "Sombreuil" and cut them for arrangements to bring indoors. When a neighbor calls to tell me she has a rose that smells like lemon and asks if I want to come over to dig up a sucker shoot, well, with uncharacteristic promptness, I drop the task at hand and go quickly, shovel and bucket in tow to begin the operation.

Back now to our cautionary tale. If the foregoing descriptions of a little of what happens to a novice rosarian does not alarm you, then possibly you are ready to sally forth into the prickly issues of growing roses for yourself. Just bear in mind that one's response to Old Garden Roses will defy all laws and reason.

Believe me.

Gardening Tomes

When *Homegrown* editor, Judy Barrett, asked me to write about my favorite gardening books, I jumped at the opportunity knowing that it would mean spending some pleasant time browsing through my garden library. The volumes dedicated to gardening collected over many years, number several hundred, a tally I never focused on until now. Shelves mounted on the wall above my writing station contain the books within easy reach to check a point or provide inspiration. Having grouped them by subject allows for their quick location, but makes it difficult to keep a tidy arrangement. As one section outgrows its allotted space, oversized books must turn on side, and smaller, thinner ones rest horizontally on the top edges of others or be jammed to fit into any vacant spaces. The overall effect resembles a jumbled disorder such as that found in vegetable gardens at end of season.

Selecting favored books at first might seem an easy task. In fact, it poses unforeseen challenges because the "favorites" amount to far too many to name here. Scanning the book spines for titles, then removing volumes to reexamine their contents, affirms the owner's fondness for them and divulges a few of her habits: bright stick-em tabs with scribbled notes mark previous references. Furthermore, shameless highlighting in yellow or green of entire paragraphs; torn scraps from once-relevant stationery sheets tucked here and there; remarks or observations penciled on endpapers; and scented cards inserted among the pages, together with bits of ribbon or found bird feathers signal noteworthy passages.

So, how first to choose? For frequency of use? For portability? A start-up, bare bones, core collection? Or, the never-to-live-without-books-one-would-rescue-in-case-of-fire? An answer comes in a moment of quiet reflection by recognizing that the proposed titles should represent something of each of the above. Yet most of all, the selection must offer reliable reference, and, of course, the joys of continuous refreshment. Here then, a partial sampling of my favorite gardening books, and the reasons for choosing them:

For Reference

A Practical Guide to Edible & Useful Plants, by Delena Tull published by Texas Monthly Press. This book does exactly what the title suggests. Totally reliable, it contains recipes, information about toxic plants, ways to make dyes, and how to use plants in interesting ways. This book I would take on an adventure hike, much like having Delena Tull herself along as a most valued member of the expedition.

Dictionary of Gardening comes in 4 volumes and is edited by Mark Griffiths and published by the Royal Horticultural Society. Aside from my sentimental attachment to them as treasured gifts from my parents, I consult these hefty volumes first when wanting to learn about the history and cultivation of plants. If able to carry them, no question they would come with me in case of fire.

How to Grow Vegetables & Fruits by the Organic Method is edited by J. I. Rodale and published by Rodale Press. Purchased decades ago from a used bookstore, I have yet to find anything to equal it for scope or depth of information. Particularly useful because the information applies anywhere in the country, and it meets the bare bones, start-up, core-collection test.

For Refreshment

A Garden Story, by Leon Whiteson and published by Mercury House could be subtitled *A Love Story.* With refined sensibilities, Whiteson elegantly recounts his awakening to a love of horticulture, using the "metaphor of the garden as a lover's heart." He came to gardening by accident, and late in life, as I did. Every page resonates, giving voice to personal joys and reflections.

The Metamorphosis of Flowers by Claude Nuridsany and Marie Pérennou and published by Abrams has photographs alone that take the breath away, and the text reads like poetic prose. Pure magic.

Trees, A Celebration is edited by Jill Fairchild and the publishers are Weidenfeld & Nicolson. In this slender volume the editor responds to the desecration of trees over the planet by celebrating their being. Presented in anthology form, she has compiled short, diverse pieces drawn from the literature of the centuries. The reader feels united in spirit with the writers, uplifted and alive. This book is illustrated with lovely woodcuts.

Chapter 7
Plant Apologia

Just a Weed? The Dandelion

> Perhaps if we could penetrate Nature's secrets we should find
> that what we call weeds are more essential to the well-being of
> the world, than the most precious fruit or grain.
> —Nathaniel Hawthorne

One of the most readily identifiable and and under appreciated plants in the world, the common dandelion, is one especially enjoyed by children. After the dandelion's yellow ray flowers have withered, the smallest child can take the remaining puffball seed heads in hand, blow on them and joyfully watch the tiny, white downy parachutes disperse in air.

The array of common names bestowed on the dandelion suggests something of the plant's more whimsical qualities or uses. Take, for example, a few of these: lion's tooth, blowball, monk's head, milk witch, wet-the-bed, swine's snout, Irish daisy, telltime, peasant's cloak, yellow Gowan, heart-fever-grass.

The reference to lion's tooth probably derives from the shape of the leaves, which are deeply grooved and jagged, medium green, and emerge from the root to form a rosette at the surface. With origins in the Mediterranean regions of Europe and Asia Minor, and with recorded references dating to 300 B. C. , dandelions were given the Latin name *Dens leonis* by the fifteenth-century German surgeon Wilhelmus. Since then the French called the plant *dent-de-lion* (lion's tooth), leading eventually to the English modification, *dandelion*.

The name monk's head refers to what's left of the little flower after the spent flowers form the tiny seed parachutes. Once dislodged from their host, the parachutes leave a bald, round surface which has been likened to the shaved heads of monks—like a pate. Swine's snout owes its name to the way the flower looks when closed.

But children's joy and such imaginative names notwithstanding, dandelions mostly are considered weeds and often targeted for eradication. Gardeners seeking weed-free flower beds and vegetable plots will go after dandelions with a vengeance. Some homeowners go mad at the effrontery of dandelion puffballs interrupting the green expanse of their otherwise placid lawns and set about to eliminate them systematically.

Regrettably, in these cases what gardener-homeowners don't know hurts them, for the common dandelion is an indicator of the health of the soil. According to Ehrenfreid E. Pfeiffer's *Weeds and What They Tell*, dandelion is a dynamic plant which influences its surroundings. Earth-worms gather round the soil near dandelions, and because these plants can produce roots three feet deep, they act as "root-channels" by transporting minerals, especially calcium from the deeper layers—even to hardpan—and bringing them to the surface. Pfeiffer says that when the dandelion dies, its root-channels act as "elevator shafts" for the earth-worms: "It 'heals' therefore what the soil has lost, what has been washed downwards."

Dandelion's healing properties extend to medicine and food as well, and the plant has been in use for over 1,000 years by ancient Egyptians, early Greeks, the Chinese, and by Arab physicians of the Middle Ages. As medicine, dandelions have been used to treat ailments of the liver, gallbladder, and spleen; as a diuretic; as treatment for consumption and eye disorders: and as antibacterial and antifungal agents, among other uses. Dandelion's scientific name, *Taraxacum officinale*, (from Greek *taraxos* for disorder and *akos* for remedy) seems to acknowledge these properties.

As food dandelions represent one of the most nutritious vegetables in existence with their high vitamin and mineral content: vitamins A, B_1, C, calcium, niacin, riboflavin, protein, iron, phosphorus, and potassium. The roots, leaves, and flower buds may be consumed in a variety of ways. Roots may be made into coffee; leaves may be eaten in salads (raw or cooked); and the flowers fermented for use in dandelion wine. The flowers also make a yellow dye, and using the entire plant will produce a rich magenta dye.

Dandelions even offer beauty benefits as a handful of flowers infused in water and strained are said to have been used long ago by European women to rid their skin of freckles.

Endowed with these many beneficial attributes, it is a wonder that dandelions have been so maligned by unknowing gardeners. Perhaps they would be willing to reconsider this simple plant if they knew that magical properties have been ascribed to it. For instance, in her book *Just Weeds* Pamela Jones cites the 16th century naturalist Matthiolus who records magicians claiming that "If a person rub himself all over [with dandelion], he will everywhere be welcome and obtain what he wishes."

Who could wish for anything more?

Doctor Culpeper and the Butterfly Rose

Roses have almost universal appeal for many reasons: their sumptuous blossoms, varied color, seductive fragrance, and their perennial vigor. Some may be appreciated as mannerly climbers while others may be valued for their apparent wildness. Roses can be commonplace or rare, but of all flowers they perhaps are the most easily recognizable.

Roses have served as symbols through the ages: as emblems of war, of peace, of secrecy. The ancient Romans, for instance, would hang a rose from chamber ceilings if they wanted confidentiality—hence the term *sub rosa*. Or, as ambassadors in amorous adventures, roses have dispatched messages of bashful affection, of jealous and passionate love, of tranquility, of purity. That many Old Garden Rose varieties have historical significance is evidenced by the majestic foreign names sometimes assigned to them ("Duchesse de Brabant," "Souvenir de la Malmaison").

Although for the most part roses have had their legions of steadfast admirers, there have been persons of more reserved opinion; notably Nicholas Culpeper who in the 17th century declared in his *Complete Herbal and English Physician*: "What a pother have authors made about Roses! What a racket they have kept!" While he does go on to cite the many "good sundry uses" for roses, he confines his appreciation to their medicinal, rather than their aesthetic values.

Each to his own, of course. Yet it is a pity that the dyspeptic Doctor Culpeper could not have been transplanted into our own century when he might have enjoyed the charms of the many "modern" roses cultivated today. His disposition might have noticeably improved on observing the exuberant blooming of *Rosa mutabilis*, for example, the vigorous shrub rose from China, which dates probably from sometime prior to 1894.

Its name, meaning "changeable" in Latin, alludes to the ever-changing colors of the blossoms that cover the entire bush. The open-faced flowers each have five flexed petals that darken in the sun as they mature and bear a prominent center crown of golden stamens. Colors range from buds in brilliant orange to fully formed flowers in creamy yellow, rich apricot, salmon, mallow pink, and rouge. To see such a mass of colorful blooms on a bush that can grow seven feet tall and five to six feet wide or more takes the breath away. Small wonder that Butterfly Rose is its common name, for the flowers appear to fasten onto the narrow, bronzy leaves like butterflies, causing one to worry that they might flutter away at any moment.

Unless he could have experienced the effects of Butterfly Rose firsthand, Doctor Culpeper surely would have dismissed such praise as effusive. As a physician and a scientist no doubt he would have remarked that excessive summer heat and alkaline soil might affect the rose's performance somewhat. And likely he would have noted that the flowers have little fragrance and would have cautioned against planting it any-where temperatures fall below 10° F. But if he could have observed its overall health and vigor, its apparent immunity to pests and diseases, he might have been willing to pronounce it an outstanding specimen plant. If only he could have seen how it enlivens a Southern garden, blending so well with other plants, he might have joined in with the general euphoria.

A Curiosity: The Chinaberry Tree

It is puzzling to me that a perfectly beautiful tree, validated by time and admired by some of our country's "greats," should be disdained and considered a pesky weed tree by many people today—the chinaberry tree. Was George Washington misguided in his decision to plant chinaberry trees at Mount Vernon? Did Thomas Jefferson—passionate and informed gardener that he was—suffer an uncharacteristic lapse of judgment when he included chinaberries in a planting of ornamental trees at his beloved Monticello? What about Henry Wadsworth Longfellow evoking the shores of the Mississippi River "Shaded by china-trees, in the midst of luxuriant gardens," in his tragic Acadian tale *Evangeline*? For one more example, consider *Uncle Tom's Cabin* in which Harriet Beecher Stowe describes "a noble avenue of China trees, whose graceful forms and ever-springing foliage seemed to be the only things . . . that neglect could not daunt or alter,—like noble spirits, so deeply rooted in goodness, as to flourish and grow stronger amid discouragement and decay."

Those illustrious Americans willingly joined the ranks of individuals who appreciated the chinaberry's "graceful forms and ever-springing foliage." A few hundred years earlier, in the 16th century, the chinaberry was planted as a street tree in England. Before that, it had near legendary status as an object of worship in Ceylon, Malaya, and Persia. More recently, it was planted along public boulevards and avenues in the southern United States, where it was once considered a desirable shade tree.

What has happened in the intervening years to eclipse the china-berry's favored place in the sylvan world is unclear. Only infrequently now is its wood used for cabinetry or for firewood; its bark and leaves no longer are prized for their medicinal qualities, or the fruit pulp decocted for use as an organic insecticide against cutworms. Now pungent, chemical moth-balls are chosen to protect fine clothing during the winter months instead of the berries of the chinaberry tree.

Despite this modern day neglect, the chinaberry (*Melia azederach*) has a patrician lineage. It is a member of the mahogany family [Meliaceae] and its species name, *azederach*, is a Persian word meaning "noble tree." The chinaberry's other common names give some idea of its worldwide distribution: Persian lilac, pride of China, Indian lilac, Syrian bead tree, Japanese bead tree. Some sources state that it is a native of Northern India and China; other references suggest Syria and Southeast Asia. Chinaberries are said to have been introduced into European cultivation by Greek monks who used the dried seeds for prayer beads.

The chinaberry's characteristic rapid growth to about medium size and its wide-branching crown make it valuable for reforestation in its native regions. The arrangement of glossy, dark green leaves looks like giant feathers; they begin to unfold just as the flowers appear in spring. Fragrant, lilac-colored flowers with dark purple stamens hang in loose panicles. The clusters of yellow berries are toxic to humans, but many songbirds, especially robins and mockingbirds, feast on them when they ripen in the fall.

Zoned for regions 7-10, chinaberries tolerate a range of well-drained soils and hot, dry conditions. This fact alone might suggest a renewed interest in chinaberries for use in xeriscaping. The chinaberries we have growing on a south-facing bluff at our Brazos House garden, for example, have survived brutal droughts without any extra watering efforts on our part. This species, known as the Texas umbrella tree (*M. umbraculi-formis*), is very hardy. As the common name suggests, its shape is rounded like an open umbrella. The species was discovered in 1894 near San Jacinto battlefield.

As an ornamental, chinaberries provide appealing textural and structural variety to the landscape—the same effect Thomas Jefferson wanted to achieve. Although deciduous, their leaves turn a buff yellow in the fall before dropping. The leaves and the clutches of yellow berries appear together and are a welcome addition to other trees at that time of year. The thin, slightly wrinkled, brown-red bark catches the eye and is appealing to touch.

With so many attractive qualities it does seem curious that the chinaberry is not more widely appreciated or recommended. Some of the lack of modern-day interest may be due to the chinaberry's relatively short life span, its weak wood which is sometimes easily damaged, and its tendency to sprout up everywhere from fallen seed.

But the shortcomings of chinaberries seem minor when compared to their many benefits and special beauty. Recall how Harriet Beecher Stowe perceived their uniqueness: "It was a superb moonlit night, and the shadows of the graceful China trees lay minutely penciled on the turf below."

Chapter 8
Vegetable Favorites

For Radishes

Like everyone else, gardeners sometimes need a little instant gratification. Especially when growing vegetables—that arc of time from seed sowing to harvest—can seem too long. Packets of seed purchased early in the season at a neighborhood nursery or on a whim from the grocery store kiosk are examined hurriedly for instructions on "When to Plant," for germination times, and for "Days to Maturity." Anything that *germinates* in seven days or less promises to be rewarding, and whatever *matures* within a mere four weeks will merit priority placement in planning for the annual spring vegetable garden.

Radishes offer these and other advantages as well. Most varieties suitable for spring planting ("Champion," "Cherry Belle," "Sparkler") germinate in four to seven days and mature within 22 to 28 days, making them a perfect choice for an area that can be given over to something else later. To sow seed on a Saturday afternoon, and then to see the first seedlings emerge by the following Friday is always gratifying. This makes them fun for children to grow as they learn the gardening arts, for they can see almost immediate results, and even their tiny fingers can handle the small, round seeds. And since radishes are practically mistake proof, they can also help the adult gardener recover from certain other gardening mistakes, such as having taken an exalted view of one's abilities by trying to grow artichokes during a Texas heat wave.

Radishes redeem garden failures because they behave so well, their pert tufts a welcome sign of spring. Their quick emergence allows planting them to mark rows of carrots or to ring mounds of squash seeds. Thinning the seedlings is a pleasant task, and the removed seedlings may be used in salads or in soups. When young and tender, the leaves may be eaten, and the smooth, round, red globes offer up a range of eating possibilities. If left in the ground too long, radishes lose their crispness and become woody. But even at this stage they can exhibit positive behavior because the seed pods, like miniature snap peas, make tasty additions to stir fries.

Nutritionally, radishes possess high levels of potassium, yet remain low in fat and calories. We serve up our garden radishes sliced into thin rounds, mixed with mandarin oranges and lightly placed over fresh spinach drizzled with that famous movie star's fabulous bottled dressings. We also enjoy following a European custom by placing radish slices on open-faced buttered French bread.

Although their botanical name *Raphanus sativus* sounds like the name of an emperor from ancient Rome, it nonetheless places radishes firmly in the Cruciferae, or cabbage family. Radishes are believed to have originated in the Eastern Mediterranean and by 2000 BC became an important food crop for the Egyptians. Their cultivation spread to China about 500 BC, then to Japan by about 700 AD. The Oriental variety of radish, referred to as daikon, are long-season radishes that are best planted in late summer or fall as they require longer maturing times.

With emergence almost guaranteed, radishes might be considered a fail-safe vegetable. They extend a measure of security to gardeners in this uncertain world, bringing to mind American essayist E. B. White's classic remark in a letter to a friend: "Our vegetable garden is coming along well, with radishes and beans up, and we are less worried about revolution than we used to be."

Tomatoes
(Part I)

Give someone tomatoes fresh from the garden and you may gain a friend for life. Even persons not inclined to showing appreciation are often transformed with gratitude when presented with a small basket of tomatoes still warm from the sun. The round fruits heaped together are admired as gentle fingers slide smoothly over the glossy flesh. Perhaps the recipients are a little embarrassed, having been observed making such a tactile gesture, benign though it is. They smell the perfect produce, examining the stems still attached (proof of a *real, homegrown* tomato.). This prompts folks to relate memories of incomparable tomatoes ripening in a grandmother's garden where they played as children. Or how once, when possessed of a larger patch of land, perhaps someone had tomatoes they had grown to share. And now, looking at the gift basket of fresh homegrown tomatoes again, the lucky recipient will describe with touching enthusiasm just how he or she will prepare these tomatoes for tonight's dinner and tomorrow's lunch and much more.

Any lover of fresh tomatoes looks forward to the season's first abundance. Come spring we may still be rushing about to protect tender transplants from a cold snap or two, but our minds have already made the leap to an early summer harvest. We envision row after row of mature tomato plants heavy with the plump fruit. We can see a freshly cleaned trug positioned beneath the plants, filling quickly with perfect, yes p-e-r-f-e-c-t, tomatoes.

In his book *The Food-Lover's Garden* Angelo Pellegrini quotes his southern Italian friend Leonard, a skilled tomato grower, describing the perfect tomato:

> Leonard knew tomatoes. He knew that a tomato such as he could not live without had gloss, depth of color, resilient solidity, and a dense juice that does not easily separate from the pulp. 'When you bite into a perfect tomato, there is no drip,' he used to say. 'When the juice is thin and runny, the tomato is watery. And the sweetness of a tomato, its perfection of flavor, is that special kind that results from a nice balance of acid and vegetable sugar in the mature fruit.'

Many of us probably have memories of perfect tomatoes full of the flavor that Leonard describes. I have two such memories. The first is of a large platter of sliced, beefsteak tomatoes served on a summer afternoon in a family-style restaurant in north Georgia. The tomatoes were all grown "out back."Although it was some twenty-five or thirty years ago, I can remember still the yellowed crazing and delicate pink roses of the china forming a floral border around the thick, firm, and dark red slices. Everyone sat together at one long refectory table; the request most frequently heard that day was "Pass the tomatoes, please."

The second memory is of a dish of tomatoes served in a quaint village in Maryland. My husband and I had heard of a small restaurant off the beaten path which featured fresh vegetables grown organically on premises. An imaginative young chef had purchased an abandoned church property a few years before, afterwards converting it to a fine restaurant. To this day, some fifteen years hence, I can remember sitting at that romantic little table in the transept, experiencing those slices of tomatoes with the perfected balance of flavor Leonard describes. The dish was simplicity itself: slabs of creamy mozzarella interlarded among the bright red slices, the thinnest drizzle of extra virgin olive oil, all sprinkled with snippets of fresh basil.

It has been said that the tomato is America's most popular home garden vegetable. I believe this is partly because everyone knows that the best way to achieve a flavorful tomato is to grow it yourself and partly because tomatoes are relatively easy and fun to grow. We gardeners study endlessly over the determinate and indeterminate varieties, their planting methods (Trenching method? Vertical string method? Simple transplant?) and how many tomatoes of each variety to plant.

Even the laziest gardeners will take extraordinary measures to ensure the best crop. Seasoned and novice gardeners alike will hover and potter and fuss over their tomatoes. In late spring we pinch off every side shoot found in a leaf axil, and by late summer we may nip out the tops of staked plants just as the gardening authorities recommend for an extended harvest. No matter that thumb and forefingers become stained chartreuse by the tomatoes' minty juices. We will stake them, cage them, spy on them at night with flashlights for evidence of bugs, or pour the most exotic concoctions to jump-start their roots. It's a wonder we don't kill them with kindness.

All this trouble we take, yet consider what Leonard says:

> The tomato plant is a weed. It grows better neglected, without cultivation. I saw one once growing on a rock pile, loaded with perfect tomatoes. Who knows where the seed came from?

I think Leonard is right. We found a tomato once volunteering in a rose bed. We left it to grow on its own, no cage, no stakes, no pinching out, no fertilizer, nothing at all. Then one day we spotted a blush of red beneath healthy green leaves, then another, and another. The trug quickly filled, and I soon began to think about preparing those p-e-r-f-e-c-t tomatoes for that night's dinner, and the morrow's lunch, and so on and on.

Tomatoes
(Part II)

In high summer the tomato crop gardeners have longed for is in full production. Then the burning question becomes: *WHY did we have to plant ALL those tomatoes?* Was it *really* necessary to have *three* of each of *twelve* varieties? They are coming on fast. Now that the plant tags are faded from the summer sun, how do we keep track of varieties? Which is "Big Boy," "Mortgage Lifter," "Brandywine," or "Celebrity?"

This causes a hectic pace in the kitchen, too. How many ways are there to prepare tomatoes? Baked tomatoes, tomato sandwiches, tomato tarts, fried green tomatoes, canned tomatoes. We decide on tomatoes for two meals a day. Gardening friends do not want the surplus harvest since most of them, too, face the same bounty. Non-gardening friends, at first delighted with their gift baskets, have grown weary of saying thank you or of calling and asking tentatively, "Was it ya'll who left those tomatoes on our doorstep late last night?" It's a family member, though, who cuts right to the marrow with "Why go to all that trouble when you could just go to the store and buy everyone else's homegrown tomatoes?"

There are answers, of course. Such as the joy in being an active participant in that great, mysterious arc that begins with the seed and ends at the table. There is the gratification of fantasy turned reality, seeing the picture from a garden catalog become the real thing, warm and round in the hand. And we remember an explanation Garrison Keillor once gave on his *News from Lake Wobegon* radio show: He was tired of store-bought tomatoes which "taste like pink styrofoam." There also might be acknowledgment of a secret desire to be a supplier of tomatoes to upscale restaurants, or to arrange one of those tomato-tasting contests where everyone beams beatifically behind their lineups of beefsteak tomatoes.

Recall that the simple pleasure of searching for tomatoes beneath the fragrant minty leaves is as good as any Easter egg hunt with an excited three-year-old. Finding an occasional puncture in a tomato's soft, ripe shoulder is bittersweet reminder that we share this garden with our neighbors, the birds and bugs, and a Fourth of July without platters of sliced, homegrown tomatoes is positively unpatriotic.

We may respond as well that growing tomatoes offers a broad range of management styles: hands-on, hands-off, micro-manage, macro-manage, take your pick. In a fanciful mood we might even declare kinship with an orchestra conductor. With planting stick as baton, we may point to each section of the garden in turn: over there are the cherry tomatoes in unison, in the rear section the giants carrying the bass notes, here at left are the paste tomatoes, next the saladettes in chorus line, then an heirloom melody, the specialties, and so on.

Caring for tomatoes can bring forth the best nurturing and protective instincts. Blossom-end rot found at first harvest? It's a rush to the plant books, leafing through page after page of tomato pathologies to find cause and cure. Like marginal hypochondriacs, we see in every photograph of deformed tomatoes a suggestion of what could be wrong. We stare at the section on fungal disease septoria, certain that our little treasures have contracted it. A following page shows tomato leaves with irregular brown spots, symptom of early blight, yet another calamity. Yep, they have that, too. Reluctant eyes then fall on images of those freaks of the tomato world, the cat-faced specimens. With discouraged hearts we close the book and mumble something about how that's a face only a mother could love.

Fortified with the new information, we march with quickened steps to save our tomatoes. After hasty addition of organic foliar feeds and soil amendments, we step back long enough to let the tomatoes help themselves. They respond, rallying with all they've got. It is probably this wild regenerative energy that keeps us involved in tomato cultivation, and we are reminded of the tomato's genus name, *Lycopersicon,* meaning "wolf peach." Early introductions of the tomato included yellow varieties which accorded them alluring names such as *pomodoro* (Italian for golden apple) and the French *pomme d'amour* (love apple) because it was thought to be an aphrodisiac.

On this note one final response to the family member's query: I have a notion that the forbidden fruit may have been a tomato that Eve plucked from the Garden of Eden. Now that we all must earn food by the sweat of our brows, homegrown tomatoes certainly make the effort worthwhile.

Chapter 9
Garden Dyspepsia

Discontent on a Sunday Morning

A stroll through my garden usually offers respite, remedy, and repose. Not so today, for the state of the garden is displeasing and puts me out of sorts.

Disorder, decay, and chaos are everywhere. Bermuda grass has migrated to the onion rows, the zinnias have failed to reseed, nutgrass is ankle high, the okra never did come up, and the tomatoes have expired from summer's heat. With no rain to speak of for several months a fig tree has died, and the already dying "Belle of Georgia" peach tree was cut to the ground without my first having bid it goodbye. Although it is true the morning glories are now in bloom turning radiant faces to the autumn sky, the fact is they also are taking over the sweet potato patch.

While these events normally might be taken in stride, today there is zero tolerance. Not yesterday and probably not tomorrow, but today, just for TODAY, I want to see a perfectly controlled environment. Today I want ladybugs without the aphids, butterflies without caterpillars, pollinating bees without their stingers, and roses without prickles. Today I yearn for regimented rows of sturdy vegetable plants, each one dispensing flawless fruit into waiting baskets. Today Bermuda grass should not penetrate cedar borders, and vandal nutgrass should beat a hasty retreat beneath the line of garden soil. Today I want the dead fig and Georgia peach to reappear with time-lapse speed into fecund glory. And today all the flowers attending the early fall season should be most beautiful because I remembered in time to start their seed during the summer.

But, of course, nothing is that way today. Perhaps this is also because today is Sunday, and on Sundays things do seem different. Czech essayist and playwright Karel Capek has a few observations about Sundays in his book *Intimate Things*:

> Possibly there is something in the universe which does not work on Sundays and holidays and in this way the eternal order of nature is upset. It might be scientifically ascertained whether trees and grass grow on Sundays and holidays; at the same time it is an empirical fact that on the red-letter days of the calendar it rains more than other days, spiritual activity is at a low ebb, dogs smell worse than usual, and children are a nuisance; then it is windy, lots of people get drowned, and there is an excessive number of motor accidents, actors give a worse performance, trains and trams have bad service, digestions get upset and beer and literature are worse than at any other time. It is, therefore, possible that Sundays and holidays are based on some peculiar and periodical cosmic disturbance and that on Sunday mornings I simply wake up with a physical foreboding that something is not as it should be.

That's right, Karel. Things are not as they should be. Rereading my garden journal entries from Sundays of a few years back reminds me what might have been this gardening season, only reinforcing today's mood:

September 17: *Moon vine and morning glories are in full vigor. Zinnias blooming. Harvested okra, bell peppers, eggplant, tomatoes, figs, melons, and black-eyed peas. Big gully washer in late afternoon.*

October 22: *Harvested first sweet potato. Hummingbirds are gone but saw many butterflies in vegetable gardens.*

October 27: *Vegetable gardens look wonderful. Tomatoes, eggplant, bell peppers, kale, turnips, chard; all are bug free and flourishing.*

My husband approaches looking a little melancholy himself. He has found a dead house wren and has brought it for me to see. He speculates it must have flown through an open window. When it could not find a way out, he says, it probably panicked or collided with some object and died. With saddened hearts we examine the lifeless little body; there is such perfection in those delicate wings. We recall having seen a wren a day or two before, and we remark that at the time it was so pert and how bright its song.

So, it is Sunday and nothing is right with the world. A little wren is dead and my garden is a shambles. But soon peevishness gives way to remorse when realizing that the state of my garden would not have mattered to the wren. Had the wren been in the garden instead of in the house it still would be alive. It might have darted among the rampant morning glories, feasted on bugs before they could do harm, or sung its bright song from a Bermuda grass stage.

Soon tomorrow will arrive; no longer will it be today. Then perhaps the cosmic disturbance—or whatever it was—will right itself and I will once again enjoy my garden with sweeter civility.

Tulipaphobia

Ah, luscious spring, the feverish time when flowers open their petals to a warming sun, when animals gambol in fields, and people are given latitude for misspending youth dallying in the freshened air. This seasoned gardener will accord herself some slack as well, loosening her garden vest and, without the remotest concern for condemnation or contradiction, vent an opinion or two about tulips: I do not care for them. Never have. Never will.

Before explaining the reasons for such a declaration, it might be well first to reaffirm that gardeners are entitled to likes and dislikes relating to their gardens. While often it may be that they are gentle, nonjudgmental folk, beaming softly as they cradle seedlings in roughened hands with broken fingernails, it does not follow necessarily that they must love *every* plant or take them all in like small, stray animals. Gardeners can refuse a plant for their own garden if it does not measure up for them in some way.

Take professor of philosophy and garden writer Allen Lacy who asserts in his essay "Hydrangeas? Never" that "A healthy set of prejudices is a gardener's best friend. Gardening is complicated, and prejudice simplifies it enormously." He detests hydrangeas of the "bushy ornamental sorts," and states that "the dislike came first and the reasons afterward."

The same may be said for my reaction to tulips. The initial disaffection for them was immediate and visceral; later I figured out why. They seem artificial, fake, ersatz, contrived. And regularly seen in regimented rows in municipal plantings, they look trite and unimaginative. True, one might see a bee or two tumbling into the tulip's goblet-like cup, but why any insect—or human—would bother is a mystery as the tulip has no discernible scent.

Garish colors clamor for attention without the resources necessary to claim center stage. Tulips are short-lived, with no guarantee of performance beyond a single season. Not only that, but in the South, tulips must be refrigerated before planting. Imagine taking up precious refrigerator space for tulips. Once spent, tumescent tulip petals fall away like limp banana peels leaving solitary stems like green tubes standing without purpose in the ground. Then slugs or mold finish them off.

Tulips have a sordid history as well. First introduced into Western Europe from Turkey in the mid-sixteenth century, tulips became so popular that within a hundred years they were fetching prices high enough that speculators could trade in a kind of bulb futures market. The height of "Tulip mania" as it came to be known, raged in Holland between 1634 and 1637. Tulips became *the* status symbol, driving sensible gardeners to greed, causing people to pledge carriages, or even their houses to possess rare bulbs. Men went mad after amassing, then losing, vast fortunes following the inevitable economic crash.

If the tulip can be considered emblematic of cultural misfortune, it also is interpreted by some nineteenth-century florists' manuals as symbolic of fame, worthless beauty, and pride. Consider finally the first stanza of Robert Herrick's poem "To a Bed of Tulips":

> Bright Tulips, we do know,
> Ye had your coming thither,
> And fading time doth show,
> That ye must quickly wither.

Despite one's unvarnished, unfettered prejudices, I cannot help appreciating the clever, perhaps the very *best* tulip quote ever, seen on a billboard advertising a Dallas florist shop: "Tulips today, two lips tonight."

After all, there *are* those who love the tulip.

A Gardener's Lament in Summertime: Weeds

While possibly it is true that gardeners tend to be gentle folk, sensitive, generous, and kind, it also may be fair to say that there lurks within the gardener's breast the killer instinct which manifests itself most often against those garden interlopers, those green marauders known as weeds.

Weeds come into the garden much like dark thoughts, appearing unannounced, lying dormant until just the right conditions spark their emergence. Then they bully their way to the foreground, competing for nutrients of soil, light, and air. It seems they always have more staying power than the plants you choose to grow, really digging in for the long haul on their own.

Weeds will test the equanimity of even the most tolerant gardener. Troublesome and annoying, they are like the stubborn stray hair plastered across a sweaty brow, or the misplaced trowel needed at a critical moment. Unwanted and conspicuous, weeds disrupt the visual order of any carefully tended plot. Defiant aliens, brazen opportunists, they are plants without provenance or future. In short, they are the wrong plant in the wrong place at the wrong time, often provoking bitter deeds as well as bitter words.

In 1876 American journalist Charles Dudley Warner emptied his spleen on weeds thus:

> I scarcely dare trust to speak of the weeds. They grow as if the devil was in them. I know a lady, a member of the church, and a very good sort of woman, . . . who says that the weeds work on her to th[e] extent, that, in going through her garden, she has the greatest difficulty in keeping the ten commandments in anything like an unfractured condition. I asked her which one? but she said, all of them: one felt like breaking the whole lot. The sort of weed which I most hate (if I can be said to hate anything which grows in my own garden) is the 'pulsey' [purslane], a fat, ground-clinging, spreading, greasy thing, and the most propagatious (it is not my fault is the word is not in the dictionary) plant I know.

While weeds may have been the scourge of Charles Warner and his church friend, his contemporary American essayist and poet Ralph Waldo Emerson believed that the weed is "a plant whose virtues have not yet been discovered." Perhaps Emerson was more right than he knew. Consider, for example, a sampling from a current listing of so-called Useful Weeds: blackberries, mints, and violets. Then there are the alleged Worst Weeds such as bouncing bet, Japanese honeysuckle, kudzu, purple loosestrife, wild roses.

It has sometimes been suggested that what we call a weed is just a plant without a name. After all, assigning a name risks bestowing some affection on these garden pariahs. Instead, most gardeners prefer to cast a shriveling glance at the weeds, treating them as mere discards destined to be consigned to the mass grave of anonymity.

My personal approach to weeds is this: if it has a decent flower or it proves useful in some way, such as serving as host plant for beneficial insects, leave it. If it is shading or strangling something I prefer, out with it, made to retire onto the compost heap of history.

I am, in fact, grateful to the weeds, for they keep me in the garden. As a friend of garden writer Allen Lacy once said: "Weeds give purpose to a gardener's life, and justify the need to putter endlessly."

My sentiments exactly.

Compost Guilt

The compost pile languishes—a disorderly accumulation of garden debris, kitchen scraps, broken tree limbs, shredded leaves, brush, and weeds. Consigned to the topmost layers lie scattered cut flowers, their slippery stems the afterlife of arrangements set out briefly to brighten January days.

This large heap occupies a spot near the northeast end of the property behind the workshop. Curved metal fence panels restrain the jumbled contents, and a corrugated tin insert serves as backing to protect the wooden fence behind from rotting. The location provides sun enough to warm the pile, yet sufficient shade in summer from the building to prevent overheating. A hose nearby provides water, as necessary.

This unobtrusive site seems right enough for a compost pile—the visual barriers shielding any unsightliness, allowing us to compost discreetly—yet for convenience it remains proximate to household activities. Though such piles may appear lifeless at the surface, the interior teems with the complex work of decomposition: a host of organisms, bacteria, worms, insects, and fungi gather here by some mysterious, unseen bidding. Aided by heat and moisture, their synergy breaks down the raw materials, creating the humus needed for amending our gardens. In this way the soil never wears out, continually renewing itself. The earth, novelist and poet George Meredith wrote, "smells regeneration in the moist breath of decay."

Some people refer to the finished compost as "black gold," suggesting its supreme value to the gardener. The term evokes the rich, dark color; and squeezing the mixture in the palm of the hand allows an experience of its special fragrance, lightness, and "moist breath."

Yet guilt prevails regarding our compost pile because we have not been composting as we should. It has become more of a holding area where we tend to dump unwanted plant material. We forget to water or turn it as required. Worse though, for the past couple of months most of the precious kitchen scraps have not found their way to the pile.

Earlier, before we neglected the compost pile, suitable kitchen scraps were collected regularly in gallon-size stainless containers. At each day's end, I would empty their contents onto the compost pile, covering it with leaves or other debris to prevent flies. It was a satisfying task, permitting enjoyment of a sunset-filled sky while contributing to the manufacture of this earthy material for the garden. Not fulfilling this simple errand has contributed to the guilt.

At the beginning of each calendar year tradition prompts us to make resolutions; we are challenged to improve ourselves in some way. So this year, I resolve to better renew the soil by returning to the act of consistent composting.

No doubt this will assure my own regeneration as well.

A Gardener's Manifesto: Old Garden Roses

At the risk of sounding like a nettlesome gardener with too many weeds to pull, I'd like to make an appeal to stop calling Old Garden Roses OGRs.

Acronyms such as OGR are common nowadays. And they do have their place in the fields of commerce and technology: PIN (Personal Identification Number), IPA (Initial Public Offering), SAT (Satellite), PC (Personal Computer), a random sampling of acronyms which seem well-suited to the task. Two or three letters abbreviate and condense whole phrases, telling us all we need to know. In the quickened pace of today's world they supply short, energetic bursts of words for frenetic, time-stretched workers, often becoming a code for people in the know, lingo validating participation in a chosen field.

However, such verbal shorthand is not becoming to a rose garden. Is it really possible, for example, to call the voluptuous, powder-pink "Souvenir de la Malmaison" an OGR? What about "Sombreuil?" Suppose her fragrant white blossoms are bathed in moonlight. Does that produce an impulse to say, "Hey, look at that OGR in the moonlight over there?" Imagine a dining table with freshly cut Old Garden Roses composed in an arrangement reminiscent of a painting by a Dutch Master. Can we really

Souvenir de la Malmaison

A Gardener's Manifesto

Hermosa

Prosperity

Nell's Rose

New Dawn

bring ourselves to compliment the hostess by saying, "My, what beautiful OGRs you have?"

Not only their individual names, "Duchess de Montebello," "Surpasse Tout," "Quartre Saisons," "Rose des Peintres," but even the classes of Old Garden Roses have a refined ring—Gallica, Damask, Alba, Centifolia, Portland—suggesting history, mystery, adventure, allure. The multiple syllables linger on the tongue filling the head with images of nodding, scented blooms. We *mustn't* call them OGRs.

The presence of the Old Garden Roses, their style, fragrance, feel, and beauty recall more elegant times when people wore kid gloves, drove in horse-drawn carriages, ate their meals on china, sipped from crystal glasses, and left visiting cards engraved with their full names on silver trays. Those were not the days of OGRs; those were the days of Old Garden Roses.

Perhaps OGR really stands for something else. It might mean Old Guard Roses, roses of the old school. Roses that take their proper place in the garden, do their duty by blooming freely in season, show themselves in the best light, are self-sufficient, and mannerly in their habits. It would be impertinent to call them OGRs. Old Garden Roses somehow seem the most appropriate name.

Granted, Romeo and Juliet thought too much importance was attached to names. And well they might have thought so. Being born into a blood feud between names like Montague and Capulet does not a happy romance make:

> What's in name? That which we call a rose
> By any other name would smell as sweet.

Shakespeare's point of view notwithstanding, surely it is time to protest. Gardeners of the world, unite. Throw off the chains of acronyms. Say it loud, say it clear; OLD GARDEN ROSES, OLD GARDEN ROSES, OLD GARDEN ROSES, or refer to each one, as it deserves, by its original traditional, romantic name.

Spring Cleaning

Time for a few changes around here. Amid all its burgeoning, spring also brings with it a need for order, for restoring one's sense of well-being, for renewed vigor. Slough off the old and make way for the new, as plants do in spring.

A glance about the potting shed inspires such activity: it needs a major purge, a long overdue cleanup. A daunting task this, for the space is crowded to overflowing with bottles and canisters, half-closed sacks of soil amendments, blending containers, rusted watering cans, trugs, and tools— some hanging properly by hooks, some thrust into the pea gravel floor for "cleaning," others placed hastily or leaned randomly against pegboard walls.

The wooden shelves are grainy with bits of soil, sand, or scattered seed left carelessly on the surface, and they are spotted here and there with liquids spilled while mixing some exotic potion for application in the garden. The countless books and binders squeezed, pressed, or stuck together to maximize space show deteriorated spines with titles now faded from sun and heat. Removing one binder from the shelf reveals a mud dauber's nest securely fixed to the back wall. No telling how long it's been there.

Quick inspection of the tools means jettisoning about half of them, owing to age or poor condition. But then the question of replacing them arises, as many are essential to the work in the garden. And selecting a good gardening tool is no haphazard business; it requires careful thought and attention, for a quality tool becomes an extension of the gardener himself. Such a selection process takes a lot of *time*, the one resource most gardeners have precious little of, especially in spring. Nevertheless, out go the irreparable tools, while those remaining will have any dents or bends repaired if possible, and then will be properly cleaned, oiled, and stored for use again.

The real challenge comes in sorting through the plastic carryall residing on a back shelf. It contains a jumble of mismatched gloves stiffened by caked mud (some with missing finger ends), wadded plastic caps once used to tent tender seedlings, bits of knotted twine, broken hose-end connectors, a tape measure that won't snap shut, and glitter pencils in assorted neon colors, once bought in the hope of making garden note taking more appealing. Silly notion. Besides, all the erasures have gone hard, and a spider has formed a soft white cocoon next to a lime green pencil. I am overjoyed to retrieve a favored French folding harvest knife, but saddened to discover its broken blade tip. Honing the metal might restore its shape, and a coat of lemon oil no doubt will revive the luster of the wooden handle.

More rummaging produces not just one or two, but *five* seeders—all looking and working pretty much alike—supposedly meant to eject tiny seeds one by one for easier planting. Why on earth they have been kept when having to give up on them after first use? It was much less trouble to pick the seeds out individually from the palm of the hand. Next go the bottles of old, dried up liquid seaweed, fish emulsion and, root stimulator; their easy disposal is a reminder of the wisdom in gardening organically.

Pitching the deflated and cracked kneeling pad chewed by the dog during a moment of puppy mischief reminds me that weeding needs to be done, and brings to mind artist and author Clare Leighton's observation that "The tidying of the garden is as exacting and unending as the daily washing of dishes." The same might be said for clearing up the potting shed.

And the work has just begun.

Mum's the Word: Chrysanthemums

There comes a time when a gardener should confess to a plant prejudice or two to come clean, make a frank admission. Here it is then: chrysanthemums do not occupy top tier on my list of favored flowers. In fact, I secretly dislike them. Perhaps an explanation is in order.

Mums appear so frequently every fall that it seems they are the seasonal flowers of choice. Usually seen displayed in wicker baskets fastened with oversize bows, mums monopolize the autumn floral shop windows. Or they form tight borders in grocery store aisles, making it difficult for shopping carts to pass freely. In the nurseries vast areas of mums in sunset colors populate bedding plant tables often to the exclusion of other colorful flowers appropriate to the season. And on corporate lawns, pools of mounding mums pumped up with synthetic fertilizers spell out logos, or signal the entrances to retail centers.

But there's more. The common garden (or florist's) *Chrysanthemum* once had its genus name changed to *Dendranthema*. Hardly an easy word to pronounce, it sounds like a skin condition or psychic disorder. The new name came about some time after World War II to distinguish the florist's chrysanthemum from related groups such as shasta daisies, marguerites, tansies, and pyrethrums. This caused so much confusion that the earlier and more popular usage prevailed, and their scientific name *Chrysan-themum* was restored by an international committee charged with the rulings on botanical nomenclature. Chrysanthemums are divided into two basic groups: the garden hardy and the exhibition mums, with the exhibition mums further divided into 30 sections according to bloom time, form of bloom, color, and size. National and international chrysanthemum societies have held competitions resulting in an astonishing array of plant forms including trees, topiaries, hanging baskets, and bonsai. And the blooms themselves are divided into different forms such as incurved, reflexed, intermediate, anemone-centered, singles, and pompoms. Leafing through books containing photographs of some of these exotic flower heads brings to mind the organic beauty of colorful undersea creatures.

Unconditional respect and admiration should be extended to gardeners who can render such blossoms for they are faced with quite daunting maintenance tasks. Feeding, staking, spraying for pests, protecting from the effects of weather, and decisions about when and how to disbud—these are the stuff of heroic effort far beyond my gardening abilities. To reinforce this point I found one reference source containing not just one, but *five* encyclopedia-style pages on cultivation alone.

Now for another confession: some dozen chrysanthemums do exist in our garden. Despite my own prejudices I planted them in the cutting garden several years ago for a couple of reasons. The first was a practical one having to do with wanting to fill vacant spots before an important outdoor event. In this case personal conviction gave way to personal pride because the mums provided a solution for quickly achieving an impressive display of colorful, dense cover.

The second reason really was more of a rationale for the first because chrysanthemums do have a certain historical interest. Evidence suggests that chrysanthemums were grown in China as early as 500 BC. Confucius wrote about them at about that time. To have flowers bearing such ancient lineage occupying space in our garden did have its appeal.

One final note. While mums in this country have cheerful associations, in many parts of Asia and Europe they symbolize death, and used, in fact, only at funerals or at gravesites. Is it any wonder then that Hungarian-born actress Zsa Zsa Gabor is said to have thrown a fit when some well-meaning American admirer sent her a large bouquet of mums?

Mum's the word, Zsa Zsa.

Chapter 10
Garden Lessons

Comeback Rose: The "Mermaid" Rose

Portions of humble pie appear on our plates occasionally. Lessons in humility come in various ways, ours this time comes in the form of a horticultural lesson delivered by one astonishing rose.

A review of the facts: Some twenty years ago we planted the rose "Mermaid" along a rail fence on the brow of a bluff at the southwest end of our Brazos House gardens. We selected this site in part because Mermaid's thorny reputation suggested prudent placement in a more remote area of the property away from high traffic areas where its vicious, reverse-curving prickles would not snag unknowing visitors. Also, we wanted to establish a living fence and gain some quick landscape decoration in a difficult planting area.

We watched in amazement as within a few years Mermaid developed into a fence row extending 45 feet across, effectively covering what we had wanted to camouflage, but also creating an impenetrable thicket. Each May and June it offered up an arresting display of luscious, lightly fragrant, saucer-size, yellowish-white blossoms with deep golden stamens. It became an impressive sight.

As the years passed, that part of the property came to be known as "the Mermaid area," thus fixing in our minds with compass-like precision a point of reference. We grew accustomed to the rose's formidable presence, looking forward each season to its spectacular show. But over time a nagging concern arose about giving that particular spot entirely over to Mermaid despite its flowering performances and exceptional vigor.

Relinquishing the area to Mermaid meant diminishing a view of the lake beyond.

Moreover, the passage of time had begun to affect mature Mermaid's general appearance, though not its vigor. The cumulative effects of abusive winds from the lake on its head-high branches, and shading from overgrowth nearby had caused considerable leaf loss at its base, exposing year round the bare, multiple trunks that by now had grown to several inches in caliper. Mermaid appeared top-heavy and ungainly, looking as if it might topple over the fence rails rather than drape along them gracefully.

These factors influenced a January decision to cut the rose back severely when some tree removal work was being done elsewhere on the property. Mermaid had grown so large that, knowing the considerable difficulties entailed in handling it, we were reluctant even to ask the arborist for a bid. To our relief he agreed to the task, stating he had dealt with these same roses on previous jobs.

When pruning day came, some ambivalence caused second-guessing of our decision. But we went ahead with it, forced because of Mermaid's colossal size to take prompt action. The arborist and his helper devised a clever method using ropes and pulleys to yank its mass of thorny foliage out and away from them as they cut. Despite precautions Mermaid was not tamed without a fight, ensnaring the two men, grabbing their shirts and hair, eventually turning any bare arms into bloody messes.

With the grim task complete, the remains of Mermaid stood posted at the fence rail looking no longer like the extravagantly vital specimen rose, but as a pathetic collection of bare, four-foot-high sticks emerging awkwardly from the ground. Fully 90% had been cut and hauled away. Remorseful at the sight, we wondered at what we had done. But Daniel, the arborist, assured us that Mermaid would return.

Indeed he was right. By end of February a few leaf sprigs began to emerge from the bare sticks, by March there were whole healthy stems with leaves, and by April it was clear that Mermaid would recover fully to sport once more her blossoms in this, her first comeback season.

Lesson learned.

Garden Rx

From time to time unexpected things can and do happen in a garden. If they arouse wonder, are difficult to understand, or seem inexplicable we may attribute them to Mother Nature's mysterious ways. If they cause problems needing quick solutions that reside outside known procedures we have to rely on conjecture or personal experience for remedies. Sometimes we might use a mixture of both, as has occurred here.

Erecting a pergola for us on the property many years ago, a workman dropped a cedar log onto a prized climbing rose seriously damaging its main stalk. Scrambling to save the rose, I gathered together the only things at hand at the time: petroleum jelly, an old palette knife, and green plastic nursery tape. With this improvised rescue kit I proceeded by using the knife for applying generous globs of petroleum jelly to protect the wound from insect marauders. Then, carefully fitting the broken but still green sections together, I bound them securely with the nursery tape and smeared any excess jelly onto the outside of the bandage as additional pre-caution. What inspired such a makeshift operation remains a mystery to this day. Possibly photos of elaborate grafting techniques seen in books came to mind. In the urgency of the moment this procedure was a practical response to an unfortunate accident. I believed that it might work and hoped the rose would heal itself in time.

Removing the green bandage several months later the stalk appeared fully restored. Though somewhat scarred by a large, protruding scab that had formed over the area of joining, the injured stalk had healed completely. The rose flourished with healthy new leaves and sumptuous blooms despite a few galls that had appeared along the stalk in several places where none existed before. It seemed a full recovery.

A similar situation occurred while planting a live oak tree. A small branch had been broken during transport prior to planting. Normally, to tidy overall appearance after an accident it is customary to prune away any unsightliness or injuries. But this branch faced the main viewing direction and, though still young and slender and about twice the diameter of a pencil it had the potential of forming into an important limb offering graceful structure with some spreading shade. For these reasons we resolved to try to save the branchlet, using the same technique devised for the rosebush some years before.

However, this time different conditions caused some concern whether the procedure would succeed. Unlike the rose stem still very green after the accident, there had been a lapse of time before we discovered the break on the tree. Consequently, the broken sections had begun to dry, and only a small sliver of bark held the two parts together. This would make binding them more difficult and would narrow the chance for success. It seemed worth a try nevertheless.

The wrapped and jellied treatment remained in place for about six months. During that time healthy new leaves formed and the branch seemed stronger. Surprisingly, it withstood some heavy winds which blew for many days.

Occasionally I removed the bandage long enough to check progress: the split in the bark still was evident, but it appeared that some healing had occurred. After about nine months the limb was still tender but the prognosis seemed good.

About five years have passed since applying this makeshift remedy. Today the live oak stands with its damaged branch now whole—a scar still identities the spot where the tree healed itself without its protective bark. The affected branch extends in all its beauty with leaves and acorns like the tree's other strong limbs.

Spring Admonitions

An antique edition of Robert B. Thomas's *The Farmer's Almanack* (1809) contains these urgent exhortations for the month of March:

> Delay not to ſet your things in order. An inactive ſlothful man is good for nothing on a farm. Do you not ſee the ſeaſon for buſineſs faſt approaching? Where are your tools of huſbandry? Is your corn ſhelled? Is your flax got out? See to pruning your fruit trees. Don't ſet in the houſe and lounge about the fire, with your brains drowned with the fumes of cynder; while your neighbors are all alive with buſineſs about you.

And for the month of April:

> How happy is the farmer who has been wiſe during the laſt winter, and has not ſlept away his hours in ſloth and inattention, like a bear in a den. . . . His heart is cheerful—he is brave, active and lively. Strength is in his bones, and labour is his delight all day long.. . . Your ploughing, I preſume, is all done, if not, ſpur up the boys and haſten to buſineſs. I tell you ſeriouſly, there is not a moment in a day which a farmer may not improve to much profit.

So it seems there existed even in those labor-intensive days of the early nineteenth century procrastinators and couch potatoes.

Yet the call to garden activity in the spring months is a natural thing. We have enough to say grace over without Mr. Thomas's militant prodding to do this, do that. Nor have we here "slept away our hours in sloth and inattention" for, after all, each year we deal with what remains of our fall and winter gardens.

For example, there are the broccoli and brussels sprouts to clear away for the tomato transplants after a last freeze. Homemade compost must be worked into the soil. And the time comes to wind down harvesting the red and white cabbages to make room later for okra and amaranth. Also, we keep an eye on seedlings emerging in their starting trays in the potting shed: eggplant, squash, zucchini, cucumber, morning glory, moon vine, and hyacinth bean vine. In addition, there's the Turk's cap and rock rose that have been propagating, although somewhat less successfully.

Let's not overlook the seed catalogs, or the record-keeping, either. The paperwork associated with ordering flower and vegetable seeds lies scattered about in piles because, Mr. Thomas, we have been too busy to file. We're also checking this year's garden plan against last year's to ensure proper rotation for health of the soil. Moreover, we have begun the succession planting of flower seed, radishes, and lettuce.

While we're at it, we know that nothing lays so bare the imperfections of the slothful gardener as neglected tools. So off we go to purchase a new shovel head to replace the one bent while digging in rocky soil and to haul the power mower for a needed tune-up. During slack time we'll sharpen the cutter blades on the pole pruner, then take a breather while cleaning and oiling all the tools hanging on the north and west walls of the cedar barn. Have we forgotten anything?

But know this, Mr. Thomas: our hearts are cheerful—we have been brave, active, and lively. Strength is in our bones, Sir. We have "ſet our things in order. And we haſten to tell you ſeriouſly that this labour has been our delight, all day long."

Trees

In a few days, seventeen trees will be removed from the property here at the Brazos House gardens. While removing seventeen will still leave many trees—too many, by some accounts, to have a *proper* garden—this is not a step taken casually. There are valid reasons: most of those slated for removal are old or dying, are too close to the main house, are chronic hosts to mistletoe, are being crowded out by competition from larger trees, or are so poorly situated they likely will not withstand the tests of heavy weather and time.

Author Willa Cather once commented that she liked trees because they seem more resigned to the way they have to live than other things do. Her remark offers scant consolation; the trees may be resigned but we humans are not, feeling compelled as responsible stewards to make changes we believe to be for the better.

Is it possible to miss things before they depart? To mourn before a sad event comes to pass? The questions spring to mind because within a few hours of contracting for the tree removal work, an acute sense of loss replaces an otherwise sanguine mood. Green plastic ties now mark the targeted trees making them look like bereaved persons wearing armbands to signal a period of personal mourning. To see them bent with time or disease or some other condition causes regret and a dread of what we know is forthcoming, but also prompts a renewed appreciation for what they have endured. German novelist Hermann Hesse wrote:

> When a tree is cut down and reveals its naked death-wound to the sun, one can read its whole history in the luminous, inscribed disk of its trunk: in the rings of its years, its scars, all the struggle, all the suffering, all the sickness, all the happiness and prosperity stand truly written, the narrow years and the luxurious years, the attacks withstood, the storms endured.

Trees stimulate personal introspection, moments of meditation and reflection. How easy it becomes to collect one's thoughts in the presence of trees, thereby gaining new perspectives on difficult matters. Their height allows us to stand a little taller if we should be feeling small; their girth allows for leaning when we might feel weak. Their silence speaks of an elemental intelligence, of wisdom and strength borne of endurance. Whispering seems more appropriate in a grove of trees, like being in a library. See them stand or bend against blustering winds, their leaves carried recklessly in swirling currents of air—the sight fosters the notion that if they can do it, perhaps we can withstand life's bullying moments as well.

Trees are steadfast friends. One tree in particular I shall miss, a hackberry located just outside the large window of my writing room. Now in poor condition, it has grown too close to the stone wall nearby causing concern that its roots will undermine and break the wall. A wind chime suspended from beneath one of its limbs makes audible the slightest breeze, giving sound to unseen forces. The other day a white-winged dove perched in its branches. Surrounded by the tree's berries, for a moment the dove evoked the holiday image of a partridge in a pear tree. The knots and wrinkles in the bark of this hackberry look like the sad eyes and hide of an aging elephant.

Friends such as these must be felled with reverence, not by the ax of a careless woodsman. Hear this, woodsman: the person right for this task will first pat the trunks of the trees before submitting them to the chain-saw, silently asking their forgiveness in the way medieval executioners asked forgiveness of doomed prisoners before taking their payment in coin. The person right for the task will climb the trees carefully, silently hoisting himself with ropes and pulleys and chains, then position himself among the branches with simian ease. He will fire up his saw with resolve, cutting quick and clean. He will lower to the ground each amputated limb, not shouting to his crewmen below, but instructing them in a clear and respectful voice.

After completing the grim but necessary task, he will report to the troubled owners what he heard from within the trunk of each tree: *I have lived. I am ready. Farewell.*

Chapter 11
In Memoriae

A Gardener Remembered

Gardening teaches many things, and many teachers are gardeners. One of the most inspired and best-loved gardener-teachers was Lorine Gibson, who died of a heart attack this past summer. She was 61.

Many people knew Lorine through her early career on Dallas public television (KERA-TV). Her obituary in the *Dallas Morning News* (July 10, 2002) cites her varied achievements, including her far-reaching influence as garden lecturer and editor of the *Dallas Plant Manual*.

My acquaintance with Lorine began many years ago when, through a mutual friend, Lorine invited my husband and me to one of her spring open garden days. We were enchanted by the secluded, serene, Japanese-style garden she and her husband David had created. Sandstone boulders formed a waterfall, and brilliant koi swam in spring-fed pools beneath sandstone bridges. Stepping-stones made curving paths, and the air, freshened by ferns, evergreens, and canopies of Japanese maples seemed healthier there.

Lorine strolled with us past this entry garden to "the back garden." Here she displayed, or had buried, assorted objects: little iron crosses, broken mirrors, pottery shards, miniature houses, old toys. In the sunny spots beyond were the flower and vegetable beds, splashing color within unique borders made from glass bottles, turned neck down in the soil. The lush, brightly-tinted colors here seemed unrestrained and exuberant—a marked contrast to the understated, controlled environment of the entry garden. As Lorine chatted with us she would drop to her knees occasionally to tidy up around the plantings. For me this act revealed the *real* gardener, ever mindful of anything out of place despite the distraction of guests.

The last time I saw Lorine was one week before she died. Appropriately enough, she was immersed in the pleasures of touring a private garden and garden library. At one time we were standing alone together, reviewing the owner's collection of garden books. As Lorine ran her fingers along the book spines, she would call out some of the authors or titles. Her enthusiasm and the way she lingered over the names suggested she had each of them committed already to her memory and to her heart.

A few days after her funeral Lorine's husband did a wonderful thing. He celebrated her life by celebrating her garden. On an appointed day he made the garden available, from sunrise to sunset, allowing Lorine's family, friends, and admirers to be close to her again in her own space.

It was a heartwarming day. At the entrance to the garden placed near the guest book, was a tray of freshly cut rosemary sprigs brought by a loving friend. So fitting—rosemary—Herb of Remembrance.

Many of the guests had visited Lorine's garden countless times, but on this day they experienced it in a different way. Their eyes might fix on the shadows created by the gnarled wisteria Lorine so admired, or they would just sit, quietly observing a delicate shudder of water passing from pool to pool. Fragments of muted conversations floated past: someone recalling the mantle of magnolias on Lorine's casket, chosen because these were the flowers contained in the last arrangement she made for the interior of her home.

Evidence of Lorine's uniqueness was everywhere. The back garden, containing her fascinating collection of broken, discarded, or buried objects might have had slight appeal for some, but to Lorine these objects had rich meaning, and so deserved a place of honor in her garden. She saw a beauty in them, or a symbolism that an untutored eye might overlook.

I loved her back garden for its complexity and its mystery, symbolic perhaps of life's paradoxes, its randomness, and its continuum. Here were the seen and the unseen, lightness and darkness, reflection and shadow. Yet, also, here one might share in her irrepressible spirit and her vitality.

Though Lorine is gone now, her garden, her valued instruction, and the example of her enthusiasm for life remain. Her closest friends recall that she always welcomed the cycles of nature, as expressed so beautifully in a favored passage written by Ken Druse in his book *Making More Plants: The Science, Art, and Joy of Propagation*:

I was born in the spring and I never got over it. I am obsessed by seasonal changes: am far too susceptible to the blahs as day-light hours shorten in autumn, get a little too high for my own good when the evening light lingers. I love plants—the way they look and smell, leaves crisp in the fall and flower buds bursting into bloom in spring.

The First Part of
A Tree Story

A few years ago we acquired about a third of an acre, a piece of land that expanded our existing property to allow for additional landscaping and for certain building improvements. Though pleased by how the addition would enhance the property as a whole, we recognized there would be many challenges associated with its acquisition.

For decades the lot had served as a car park, paved with four inches of asphalt over a caliche base. Several large cedar elms and a trio of post oaks stood along the fence lines that previously formed old boundaries to our property south and east; otherwise, this tract was devoid of any living thing.

We often wondered how the elms and post oaks that straddled the line shared with the car park could have survived, their roots half-starved for moisture beneath the parking lot side, or buried under an iris bed on our side. It is a curious irony that these trees should have endured such a divided existence for so long. It brings to mind a remark made by *The New York Times* gardening correspondent, Anne Raver, that "an iris likes to sit on the ground the way a duck sits on the water: half in, half out." Just so. For years we had safeguarded these half-in, half-out trees for their spreading shade.

Resolved to transform this new lot into a landscaped area that could be integrated into the entire property, we set about first to remove the asphalt and caliche. Heavy machinery pounded the asphalt to break it up, pushing it with the caliche into manageable mounds. Accretions of old pipes together with thick, contorted spirals of rusted rebar protruded from the stockpiles. And as the long neck of the backhoe reached into each mound, it would emerge gripping enormous chunks of asphalt, its saurian jaws closed shut or cocked open countless times before releasing the wreckage of pavement and rubble into the waiting transport trucks.

Completion of this heavy work left us with a real *tabula rasa*—a blank slate—so desolate and barren that it seemed a step beyond a moonscape; it seemed more a Mars-scape with a surface slab of thick, lifeless hardpan. For a while the ferrous dust caused by movement of the machinery lent a mysterious atmosphere, something planetary and other-worldly.

I had not fully understood the nature of hardpan until seeing this: the tines of a digging fork could not penetrate it and water simply pooled for days into low pockets or would run off the slanting terrain. The packed clay was so dense that in dry weather heavy trucks could pass over the same area repeatedly without rutting the ground in any way.

The next phase began by aerating several times with a back-end aerator, then applying a bio stimulant to help break down the hardpan and bring it back to life. This was followed by the spreading of many truckloads of good topsoil, compost, more bio stimulant, and the laying of sprinkler lines.

We then felt the site improved enough to begin planting grass, some nursery stock, and a selection of trees, including what we hoped would be the focal point of this new addition to our property—a large, nursery-grown live oak tree.

The Second Part of
A Tree Story

Part One of "A Tree Story" recounts the measures we took to transform about a third of an acre of land that for decades had served as a car park into a landscaped addition to our existing property. Once we felt the site was improved enough we set out to arrange for what we hoped would be the focal point of this new addition to our property—a large nursery-grown live oak tree.

We took special care in selecting this specimen tree. On a cold, rainy, mid-February day we traveled some distance to a large nursery and viewed row after row of live oaks. Toward the end of the last row, off to the side, we spotted the one we wanted. In its 100-gallon container it stood close to 12 feet tall, with a caliper of about six inches. Its branches spread evenly and gracefully in all directions forming an impressive crown. An interesting bend in the trunk and a large knot near the base lent character, hinting perhaps at the tree's past and at something of its future.

On a record-hot day in early March our tree arrived. Six people were

A Tree
Story

109

on hand to see to its relocation in its new home. Digging the hole without a machine required the use of rock bars and sledge hammers in addition to shovels to break through the hardpan. Two stout men accustomed to such hard work pounded and strained, sweated a lot and cursed a little, but managed finally to create a cavity large enough to accommodate our tree's root ball.

We watched and held our breath as the men removed the tree from the transport trailer, rough work that caused breakage on a couple of the significant branches. As the men waited for instructions for orienting the tree, it sat teetering at the edge of the planting hole. Though some of us expressed misgivings about the hard, slick sides that had been prepared to receive the tree, the addition of root stimulator and bags of mulch, together with assurances of planting guarantees and, the desperate expressions of those hot, tired workers persuaded us to accept their work and allow the tree to be planted in the prepared hole.

The live oak seemed to adapt, along with a new mesquite tree that had been planted concurrently nearby. Although the live oak showed no sign of new growth, initially the existing leaves appeared healthy. The sprinkler system provided the tree with extra water, a requirement during this time to keep the new surrounding grass sod alive. But recalling poet James Russell Lowell's remark that "a grass-blade's no easier to make than an oak," we did not relax our vigilance for some 45 days.

The Conclusion of
A Tree Story

When planted, the live oak stood some 10 feet tall. Positioned just to the west of a newly constructed studio and workshop, we liked the appearance of its graceful branches against the backdrop of cut-limestone walls and standing-seam metal roof. Envisioning it at maturity, we imagined how its massive limbs one day might shade the building from the blistering afternoon sun of North Central Texas.

For a while the live oak seemed to adapt well enough. The existing leaves remained healthy at first, though no signs of new growth appeared. Nevertheless, we felt we could rely on the root stimulator and other amendments that had been added to the planting hole, and on the assurances of the planting guarantee. We gave the tree extra water and continued our hopeful vigilance.

The Garden Revived

But within 45 days the tree showed signs of decline, with existing leaves turning brown. We were in the full flush of early spring, yet there were no new green leaves emerging. Puzzled by these disappointing developments, we phoned the planter who suggested that we give the tree more time.

"More time" forty-five days stretched to sixty, then to seventy-five, until finally we took matters into our own hands. There seemed no alternative but to dig around the root ball, excavating enough earth to see if there were recognizable problems in the planting hole.

The results of our inspection proved shocking: the tree seemed to be sitting in water. With hand pumps and other contrivances, the water was drained from the hole at the base of the tree. And no sooner was it pumped away than it returned again. What possibly could be the cause?

We puzzled, pondered, considered, and explored, until at last we realized that the excessive water was coming from a leak in the sprinkler line, which then flowed into the tree's planting hole by way of one of the trenches dug for the irrigation system. With nowhere else to go, the water collected in the live oak's planting hole. Our tree was drowning in water.

Helper Mike Hanley conceived and helped us execute a bold plan: first he wrapped the trunk to protect it, then using a rented backhoe machine, lifted the tree from its planting hole and relocated it to higher ground. The root ball was in shocking condition. Having been container-grown for so long, the tree's main tap root encircled the root ball like a boa constrictor, and the ball itself was hard as concrete. To aerate it, he tried stabbing at the hardened ball with a pitchfork—without success. After much discussion and with considerable misgiving, we decided to cut a major root in a final desperate attempt to help the tree rejuvenate after replanting.

This last was probably a mistake, bringing to mind artist and writer Clare Leighton's observation: "Transplanting trees is agitating work. Recollecting the dislocation and distress a human can feel at being transplanted into a new scene, one cannot help worrying when one moves a tree."

And worry we did. But surprisingly, within a short while the live oak began to sprout small clusters of tender new leaves. We were overjoyed, of course, and paid special visits every day, hoping to encourage the tree. The situation continued in this way for a while, and I secretly began to imagine we might, with luck, be able to decorate it with Christmas lights at year's end.

By late summer, after enduring sustained triple-digit temperatures, and despite the heroic efforts to save it, our beautiful tree died. Only nature knows when it will give, and when it will take away.

Chapter 12
Garden Variety

One Potato, Two Potato, Sweet Potato, Too

It would be hard to imagine the holiday months without sweet potatoes. Their deep orange flesh typifies autumn color, evoking bounties of fall harvests and Thanksgiving gatherings with marshmallow-topped sweet potato casseroles served up to generations of smiling kinfolk.

While store-bought, fresh, or canned sweet potatoes have their place, those cultivated in a home garden offer unequalled taste, and the pleasure in harvesting sweet potatoes brings a natural pride in sharing homegrown produce.

A strong, careful turn of a fragrant clod of earth brings forth multiple orange tubers growing unseen beneath a lush cover of large, heart-shaped leaves. The vines bear occasional pink flowers with magenta or deep purple throats that resemble morning glories, yet unlike morning glories they do not confine open blossoms only to the pre-noon hours.

Sweet potatoes (*Ipomoea batatas*) are not related to common potatoes or to yams. Instead, they are botanical relatives of morning glories, sharing membership in the Convolvulaceae family. This designation derives from the Latin *convolva*, to twine around; its genus name *ipomoea* derives from Greek, meaning wormlike, and its species name, *batatus*, is the Carib Indian or Haitian name for sweet potato.

Many ethno botanists believe that the origins of the sweet potato can be traced to South America, especially to the pre-Inca civilizations of Peru. Speculation about the origins of sweet potatoes found in the South Sea Islands was responsible in part for a theory developed by the great

Norwegian anthropologist and adventurer, Thor Heyerdahl: that ancient transoceanic contacts between distant civilizations and cultures was possible. He believed that the presence of the sweet potato in Polynesia and the common name they shared (*kumara*) with the old Peruvian Indians, provided an important clue and strong evidence that the Polynesians owed their origins to settlers from the Americas, possibly the pre-Inca inhabitants of Peru. In 1947, he set out to prove his theory by undertaking a 101-day epic journey from Lima to south of Tahiti in his famous balsa wood raft *Kon-Tiki*.

Thor Heyerdahl's theories notwithstanding, sweet potatoes are a staple crop of the North American South. They require frost-free temperatures and a long growing season—usually 100 to 150 days—making them ideal for Texas. They can be grown from slips ordered through garden catalogs, although producing your own slips from roots is possible, too. Mail-order slips usually sell in bundles of a dozen (sometimes more), and two bundles of a dozen each will produce ample quantities of sweet potatoes to last most of fall and early winter for two. Do not be put off by the wilted appearance of the slips when they arrive; they are hardy beyond belief, so plant them anyway and watch them recover in no time.

The favored variety in our Brazos House gardens is "Georgia Jet," not only in tribute to my own Georgia roots, but for their sweet, moist, rich taste and disease resistance. "Centennial" is also good, but "Georgia Jet" is now the only one we grow. Harvest sweet potatoes before frost, and take care in removing them from the ground. For all their hardiness and heat tolerance, they have tender skins, and can therefore crack and mildew if handled recklessly.

Come Thanksgiving, you may wish to serve up sweet potatoes using our favorite recipe: bake sweet potatoes as you would any baking potato. Cut in half, scoop the pulp, and mix in a pat of butter. Drizzle the top with a teaspoon of fine Spanish sherry. Then, when you present the dish at your holiday table, recite the lines composed by John Tyler Pettee:

> Pray for peace and grace and spiritual food,
> For wisdom and guidance, for all these are good,
> But don't forget the potatoes.

A Texas Summer Icon: The Crepe Myrtle

Throughout Texas crepe myrtles brighten summer landscapes with abundant blooms. These deciduous, ornamental tree-shrubs with multiple, slender trunks produce clusters of showy blossoms ranging from white to mauve to crimson over a period of 60 to 120 days, depending on the cultivars. Appearing as masses of large panicles at branch tips, the flowers have crinkled or crumpled edges similar to the thin cloth known as crepe, hence the common name *crepe* (alternatively crape) myrtle. *Myrtle* derives from some similarity to the myrtles (Myrtaceae) even though taxonomists place the crepe myrtle in the loosestrife (Lythraceae) family.

Summer showers may cause enough of the delicate blooms to fall to the ground so that streets or walkways glow with vibrant color. Although any rain in the hot months is always welcome, crepe myrtles being drought-tolerant do not require much moisture. They tolerate soils low in nutrients but should be planted in well-drained, sunny spots. In fall the leaves of most crepe myrtles turn red, while the white varieties will have yellow color. Trained as trees, most crepe myrtles will have an attractive bark that exfoliates, revealing a smooth, cinnamon, gray, or greenish surface underneath. Small black or brown seedpods appear in winter on terminal growth. Despite problems with aphids, powdery mildew, and sucker shoots, crepe myrtles excel as year-round performers in residential and commercial settings for use as specimens, hedges, screens, or avenue plantings.

In 1997, the 75th Legislature of the State of Texas formally declared the common crepe myrtle (*Lagerstroemia indica*) as the Official State Shrub of Texas in recognition of the tree's general-purpose value. In a House Concurrent Resolution it also recognized the planting of crepe myrtles by many counties and communities across Texas and recited some of the history of its introduction into the Lone Star State:

> WHEREAS, In 1857, the wife of Confederate General Sam Bell Maxey introduced the crape myrtle to Paris, Texas, and in 1916, after a fire devastated this Northeast Texas town, one of the community's first beautification projects incorporated these colorful shrubs; several years later, newspaper publisher A. G. 'Pat' Mayse further established the city's link to the plant when he sold thousands of crape myrtle seedlings for 25 cents each as Paris's residents prepared to celebrate Texas' centennial . . . .

Although *L. indica* may be a common sight in Texas now, its heritage is anything but common. Carl Linnaeus (1707-1778), father of modern plant classification, named the genus *Lagerstroemia* for his Swedish friend Magnus von Lagerström of Göteborg. Lagerström, a naturalist and Director of the Swedish East Indies Company, sent a specimen of this small tree to Linnaeus, but he died before he could make it back home to Sweden. Believing that *L.* came from India, Linnaeus added its species name *indica*.

The species, in fact, originated in China rather than India. It was introduced into North America in the 1780s by the French botanist André Michaux. Michaux had been sent to America by the French government to identify and collect new species of trees that they might be exported to help replenish French forests then depleted from wartime boat building. Michaux traveled the eastern seaboard states extensively, meeting prominent citizens of that time. He visited George Washington at his home in Mount Vernon where, by 1786, Washington cited having planted crepe myrtle there. If Michaux were alive today perhaps he would be pleased to know that there are more than 80 known species of crepe myrtle. While most are still used as ornamentals, selected species also are valued for timber and medicinal purposes, and for making dyes.

Given their history, their usefulness, and their adaptability to the often harsh conditions prevailing in Texas, crepe myrtles have become a true summer icon. They merit a prominent place in any Southern landscape setting.

A Garden Revived: The Potager, a Kitchen Garden

Our plot of earth west of the garage dedicated to vegetable gardening took on new life, a new look, and a new name a few years ago. Previously we referred to it as "the tall garden" to distinguish it from another garden plot on the property and because taller plants such as corn, okra, indeterminate tomatoes, amaranth, sunflowers, trellised cucumbers and so forth were grown there. But the area has been revitalized so that now it is identified as "the kitchen garden." This new name reflects the plantings done here, those traditionally associated with gardens that supplement activities of the kitchen.

Rethinking the more convenient usage of this garden also suggested an alternative planting scheme to achieve the most interesting layout. I was weary of growing vegetables each year in a 15 x 30 foot rectangular plot conventionally divided into wide, drab, regimented rows that soon gave over their precincts to the weeds. And I was fed up with struggling to contain plants with round metal cages whose stiletto supports quickly became bent or broken.

Because the garden lacked visual interest, it was less pleasurable to work. Our resulting inattention allowed radishes to become woody, lettuces to bolt, and insects to invade so that a lot of its produce was consigned to the compost heap. I longed for a garden that would yield better produce and allow for a happier state of *being* in the garden. The time had come for a change, and for a more inclusive garden, one that would contain more than just vegetables. It would have the amenities of flowers, fragrance, fruit, herbs, texture, color, and visual appeal.

Of course, cultivating a bit of land to supply produce for the owner is not a new idea. The origins of kitchen gardens reach back to ancient cultures with systems and techniques improved through the centuries and varying from country to country. By the 15th century the French had developed the *potager* where they combined vegetables and fruits in ornamental planting schemes.

Eager for a better-looking garden and fortified by history, I settled on creating a potager modified to suit our particular needs and interests. Step one involved working out a design on paper based on what we wanted to grow. At the southern end onions already had been planted in rows with re-seeded poppies emerging between the slips, leaving a 20 x 15 foot area to re-design in the potager style. This remaining area divided up nicely into nine individual beds: the four corners formed arcs, the center sections made into rounds, triangles, and oblongs. Walkways 18 inches wide were laid out using thick strips of alfalfa hay, serving to clearly define walk areas and to suppress weeds. The three center beds were ringed with radishes: one bed for eggplants, one for peppers, and each with space enough to support a trellised purple hyacinth bean vine for vertical interest.

The center bed contained the garden's focal point, a handsome vermilion hibiscus, with a surround of yellow crookneck squash plants. The remaining beds, planted individually in alternating rows of lettuce and Swiss chard, carrots and beets, and singly in cucumbers and tomatoes, were each edged with edible flowers—orange marigolds and violets—whose intense colors extended to opposite ends of the color spectrum. The other two beds contained assorted herbs and okra plants. For plant supports, four-foot bamboo arches replaced the round metal cages, giving a serial scalloped effect as we waited for the designated plants to mature. Nearby were our persimmon and pomegranate trees, blackberries, and straw-berries.

While this kitchen garden design might not suit anyone else, it has had the effect of energizing our own gardening efforts. The amenities we wish for are there, too. I still rush out to see it each day, and in more fanci-ful moments even imagine it to be the garden scene described by George Eliot in her novel *Scenes of Clerical Life*: "a charming paradisiacal min-gling of all that was pleasant to the eyes and good for food."

Best yet, though, it really is a kitchen garden because we can see it from the kitchen window.

Behold the Fig

Fig trees bear a patina of the past. For some they evoke pleasant memories of childhood summers in the country spent hiding with the dog behind grandpa's big backyard fig tree and of how grandma's washing machine out in the shed drained to water it. Others remember a favorite maiden aunt who never forgot to pack Fig Newtons in a lunch sack, and whose eccentric ways included fashioning aprons of fig leaves, "just like Adam and Eve," she would explain.

The fig's provenance reaches back far beyond childhood memory, beyond the earliest Texas homesteads into ancient world cultures and religions. Records suggest that figs were known to the ancient Sumerians, Egyptians, and Assyrians. There are numerous biblical references to figs in both the Old and New Testaments. And the Buddha experienced his enlightenment while sitting beneath a sacred fig tree. The prophet Mohammed is said to have declared: "If I should wish a fruit brought with me to Paradise, it would be the fig."

Figs have been a part of mankind's diet for more than 3,000 years. Their lush flavor and soft beauty had special appeal for the ancient Greeks and Romans who immortalized them in their mythologies. They favored them as food and as medicine. Before the first century A. D. Roman naturalist Pliny the Elder reported on the restorative properties of figs, advising their use for the infirm recovering from "long sickness," and to "preserve the elderly in better health." He also suggested that figs assist in keeping one looking young, with fewer wrinkles.

Figs probably originated in Transcaucasia and have long been native to the Southwest Asian and Eastern Mediterranean regions. The Phoenicians, Greeks, Romans, and Arab peoples all contributed to spreading fig culture throughout the Old World. Within Greece, fig cultivation became so important that it developed into a highly regulated industry.

Figs borrow their genus name, *Ficus*, from Latin "fig tree," and are members of the mulberry (Moraceae) family. The fruit of the common edible fig (*F. carica)* is unusual for it is an inverted flower containing both male and female flower parts. Known botanically as a synconium, this enlarged floral receptacle takes its name from the Greek word for fig, *sukon*. Our English word sycophant has its origins here: *sukophantes* "fig-shower," (later Latin *sycophanta)* refers to a gesture used by Greeks seeking favor from officials by denouncing criminals who exported figs illegally.

Spanish and Portuguese missionaries introduced figs into the New World. By 1769 Franciscan missionaries had planted them at their missions in San Diego, California. Today, California supplies the majority of figs grown in the US, often bearing such variety names as "Franciscan" or "Mission."

The varieties of *F. carica* most often recommended for Texas are "Celeste," "Brown Turkey" (also known as "Texas Everbearing"), "Alma," "Magnolia," and "Kadota." We have had Celeste and Brown Turkey in our Brazos House garden, but Brown Turkey is the only one remaining. Celeste fell victim to nematodes and had to be cut down. Brown Turkey has proven to be more vigorous, also somewhat better at withstanding the mineral salts from our watering with water from Lake Granbury.

Fig trees provide a unique appearance in the landscape with their large, deeply lobed leaves, and their unusual, succulent fruit that can be served up in so many ways: dried, pureed, tossed in salads, stews, made into preserves, or added to cakes and muffins. Best of all, they may be eaten right off the tree.

Figs have an ageless distinction, not only for their nutrition and eye appeal, but for their link to an important past.

Smilin' Like a 'Possum in a 'Simmon Tree: Persimmons

The restless stirrings of winter days spent indoors occasion frequent glances through our windows to the world outside. Tree trunks and bare branches against cinder skies form skeleton shapes with gawky bends and arches. Slender branches possess nothing more than a persistent leaf or two and move like crooked fingers in the chill breeze. Scenes, stilled and contained within their window frames, seem mysterious and serene, recalling the delicate ink paintings of Oriental masters. Such thoughts of the Far East bring to mind special fruits of the Orient: persimmons.

Once we had a pair of "Fuyu" persimmon trees planted at the edge of the vegetable garden nearest the house with branches that bowed gracefully under the weight of reddish-orange fruit. About the size and shape of medium-size tomatoes, the fruit hung from slim branches like holiday ornaments, joined sometimes together in pairs. In late autumn, the large, glossy, ovate leaves of these trees turned a spectacular orange-red mixed with some residual green, reminiscent of the marbleized paper found within the covers of a finely bound book.

Heavy summer rains would cause our persimmon trees to produce a bumper crop. Several times a week we would assess the fruits' varying stages of ripeness. Birds helped in this task by taste testing the ripest ones, leaving their beak marks as evidence. Absent the birds, for we humans, first came the color test: if the fruit had the ember glow of a wood fire, we moved to the next step, feeling each colored fruit for softness. If the flesh gave a little when pressed gently yet remained firm enough to handle, it was ripe for plucking. Harvesting often required the aid of a ladder, for many of the ripe persimmons hung out of reach at the top of the larger tree, which stood about fifteen feet tall.

Pruning shears help in cutting the persimmon from its stem rather than twisting it loose by hand because twisting may cause the calyx to pull away and remain attached to the stem.

Persimmon picking for us was a two-person job. By the time the picker has climbed the ladder, removed pruning shears from coat pocket, snagged a knit hat on a stray branch once or twice, descended the ladder to retrieve the harvest basket that fell from the topmost step, climbed the ladder once more to get arranged all over again, well, the presence of another person proves most beneficial in maintaining one's composure.

We gathered our harvest and placed the whole fruit, unwashed, into gallon-size plastic bags to freeze. This was a method passed on to us by an elderly neighbor. Since persimmons require cold temperatures to ripen fully, this idea made sense. And once frozen they will keep almost indefinitely. Later, simply remove from the freezer bags whatever is needed at the time, defrost, then wash and prepare. Preparation of the "Fuyu" variety is easy: remove calyx, peel, and section. Or cut in half and spoon out the pulp to eat.

Particularly with certain varieties of persimmons making the right selection for ripeness is serious business. The taste of some unripe persimmons can, as discovered by Jamestown settler Captain John Smith, *drawe a man's mouth awrie with much torment*. In other words, it will make you pucker. Really bad.

But when ripe they taste like food for the gods. And the sweet amber-colored pulp of persimmons may be used in countless ways: to make persimmon pudding, dessert sauce, pies, cakes, or as a good substitute for applesauce in recipes. The leaves may be used for tea; and even the wood —as a member of the ebony family—once was used for wooden golf club heads.

Persimmons are especially popular in the Southern states where people sometimes call them "simmons." In the South they are associated with opossums because these creatures love the fruit, giving rise to the expression "smilin' like a 'possum in a 'simmon tree." Little wonder they are found smiling, for the blush, taste, and texture of persimmons can make we human creatures smile, too.

Chapter 13
Garden Mystique

Of Saints and Soakers

An entry in a popular gardening almanac for July 15th reads: "St. Swithin's Day (Saint of the soakers). Eggs and apples are traditionally eaten today." Puzzling for a moment to determine whether the word "soakers" here means soaking rains or soaking hoses, I settle finally on soaking rains. But why eggs and apples? A few pleasant hours follow, researching St. Swithin (or Swithun), his curious association with soaking rains and with eggs and apples.

While much information about him remains sketchy or unreliable, a profile does emerge of a learned man of the 9th century (circa AD 800-862), chaplain to Egbert, King of the West Saxons and tutor to his son, Prince Ethelwolf. After his appointment as Bishop of Winchester in AD 852, St. Swithin became zealous in building churches and in repairing of old ones. Also during this period he built a bridge on the east side of Winchester where, according to the Britannia biographies, he would sit nearby to watch the workmen "that his presence might stimulate their industry." Moreover, he is said to have performed a miracle while supervising this work at the bridge. After workmen maliciously broke an old woman's basket of eggs, the holy man made the sign of the cross over them; the eggs became whole again, and the basket was restored.

Notable for his piety and humility, St. Swithin chose to journey on foot to visit distant areas of his diocese and preferred to invite the poor, rather than the rich to his banquets. When he died on 2nd July 862, he requested to be buried not within church walls, but to repose outside in the burial ground among the poor where "passersby might tread on his grave and where the rain from the eaves might fall on it."

For many years his wishes were followed, but monks at Winchester wanted to honor him with a shrine. When they exhumed his remains for reburial to a splendid place within the cathedral originally set for July 15th, incessant rains for forty days and nights delayed the transfer. It was said that St. Swithin was weeping in protest against this ostentation, thereby giving rise to the belief that he could influence the weather. Hence, according to a charming old rhyme from the British Isles, the weather on his festival day, July 15th, will determine the weather for the following forty days:

> Saint Swithin's day, if thou dost rain,
> For forty days it will remain;
> Saint Swithin's day, if thou be fair,
> For forty days 'twill rain na mair.

As to his association with apples, this seems to derive from the apple growers' hope for rain on July 15th. It is believed that rain on this day means the saints are christening the apples and that the harvest will be a good one; if it fails to rain, the harvest will be a poor one. No apples should be picked or eaten before this date so that the growing apples will ripen fully.

Given the hot, dry summers in our part of the country it seems fitting to invoke St. Swithin to favor us with a good soaker in July. I shall make it a point to be in the garden on his festival day this year, and shall have with me some assurance in the form of a few boiled eggs and sliced apples. Then, this homespun prayer shall I offer up:

> Dear Saint Swithin, if thou art fair,
> Bestow the rain on all who care;
> But dear Saint Swithin, thou must be told,
> That too much rain causes mold.

Fungus Among Us: Mushrooms

Mysteries may occur in any garden. Sometimes baffling, or curious, sometimes downright weird, garden mysteries often come as surprises in the most unexpected places. This usually is the case with mushrooms.

A cluster of mushrooms once appeared suddenly between a cedar outbuilding and a wooden fence beneath a jumble of assorted wood pieces kept on hand for odd jobs. Deep shade cast by the overarching branches of a nearby cedar elm prevented grass from growing there and caused the soil to stay damp with decaying leaves. In such ideal conditions the mushrooms—five or six in the bunch and in varying stages of development—stood in that alleyway like a gang in waiting.

They bore caps two to four inches wide whose surface broke into tan-brown shingles, or warts on the more mature specimens. The tallest in the clutch measured perhaps five inches high with a white ring on the upper stalk. Several in the group had curved scales that peeled away from the stem, like thin curls of soft wood shavings.

Their mysterious arrival, evidencing no past and no future, meant they likely would not last long, hence a need for quick identification. Consulting various references developed into a dizzying exercise of reading and comparing.

What emerged from this research opened a previously unknown world: mystical, magical, veiled, and a bit portentous. Classified in their own kingdom as fungi, mushrooms are organisms that lack chlorophyll. Known as mycology (from the Greek word *mykes*), the study of fungi includes yeasts, rusts, smuts, mildews, molds, and mushrooms. As mushrooms do not have a plant's structures of roots, stems, or leaves, recognition of all their key parts such as cap, warts, gills, ring, stalk, volva, universal or partial veil, is required for positive identification.

Accurate identification is crucial to determining edibility or inedibility, mildly toxic versus fatally poisonous. In addition to identifying the specimens by comparing their parts to detailed descriptions, important tests in the field such as cutting cross sections and making spore prints can certify correct identity. Spore prints are made by placing the cap of the mushroom on pieces of white and dark paper, then covering cap and paper with a jar or glass. The deposited spores will reveal their color, thus permitting safe identification in instances of look-alike, yet potentially harmful wild mushrooms.

As stand-ins for a mycological hunt in the forest, my references depicted page after page of otherworldly shapes, sizes, textures, and colors. Finally I made a provisional identification of our found mushrooms as Shaggy Parasols. But how distracting to see photos of some species of wild mushrooms such as Jelly Tooth, that have spines pointing downward like little ice crystals hanging from beneath the cap. Or others, like the Apricot

Jelly, formed of a gelatinous, rubbery flesh making them look like calla lilies in aspic.

Of course, morbid curiosity led to staring, mouth open, at pictures of poisonous wild mushrooms, some bearing ominous names like Destroying Angel, Death Cap, Alcohol Inky, Fly Agaric, and Deadly Galerina. Once, in a Colorado forest I saw a Fly Agaric. With its large, brilliant vermillion cap and white warts, everything about it seemed to scream *stay away*. And just the other day at a nearby ranch I spotted large bracket fungi growing out of the stump of an old hackberry tree. Growing in semi-circular shapes right out of the wood, and hard, like shelves, their undersides felt like moist suede. Suddenly, they released their spores in what appeared to be wisps of smoke carried into the atmosphere, even though the air was still that afternoon. Magical and mysterious.

Perhaps most mysterious of all are the Fairy Ring Mushrooms, for they have a secret subterranean life all their own through a system of delicate microscopic threads. The Fairy Ring Mushrooms appearing in our lawn every year form a circle with a patch of grass noticeably greener in the center of the circle. And each year they take up residence next to the rose called Mermaid.

Now *that's* a mystery.

Chaste Tree

We Texas gardeners, influenced by the need to find hardy yet showy, drought-tolerant plants, tend to forget this fundamental of a well-appointed garden—fragrance.

Springtime may naturally preoccupy our senses with the sights, sounds, *and* fragrances newly emerging from winter's sleep, but by summertime focus shifts to how to beat the heat. Trying to devise creative ways to find a bit of shade while plucking weeds, we succumb to summer's oppressive waves of heat. Or, we wonder at kitchen counters suddenly overflowing with the bounty of fruits and vegetables that seem to have ripened all at once. Thus distracted, the pursuit of fragrance becomes an almost forgotten objective.

Consider the chaste tree. It meets—indeed surpasses—the requirements for hardiness, sports showy, summer-blooming flower spikes (blue, white and pink), and is drought-tolerant. Moreover, it possesses leaves so uniquely aromatic that given a wider distribution it might just serve to bring the world to love.

My first encounter with a chaste tree took place at a kitchen doorway on my husband's family farm in North Central Texas. Having volunteered, or perhaps been intentionally planted many years before at the base of the steps, its mature spreading branches formed a drooping barrier, denying ingress or egress without one's first stooping a bit. That this did not become a source of irritation was undoubtedly due to its showy flowering and to the musky fragrance of its leaves that filled the senses.

On inquiry I learned that the locals always referred to it as the "shasta" tree, a pronunciation that my husband and I favor to this day for the memories it contains. It has become so ingrained in fact, that we must make a special effort to say "chaste" tree when speaking about it to others.

Roman naturalist and historian Pliny the Elder (1st century AD) first referred to the chaste tree as *Vitex*, now its genus name, in describing the annual rites held by the ancient Greeks to bring fertility to the fields by honoring Ceres, the goddess of harvests. Alice Thoms Vitale, in her book *Leaves* describes how the female celebrants were required to remain pure and chaste. She quotes Pliny's report of making their beds and pallets using Vitex leaves "to cool the heat of lust, and to keep themselves chaste for the time."

The chaste tree's full scientific name alludes to its history: *Vitex agnus-castus,* a botanical Latin teaser. *Agnus* means lamb, and *castus* means chaste or virtuous. It is beyond comprehending how those ancient females were expected to keep virtue intact while lying amid the redolence of *V. agnus-castus.* Undoubtedly their hearts would have been warmed and their minds inflamed by its beautifully aromatic foliage.

We should note another common name for chaste tree: monk's pepper tree. Not surprising, a fleshy fruit follows the flowers. History tells that as a means of easing their difficulties keeping vows of chastity, medieval monks would use the fruit as a seasoning or brew it into a tea.

Today gardeners may simply wish to select *V. agnus-castus* to revitalize their summer gardens—and themselves—by indulging in the pleasures of fragrance with this suggestion: place the soft, five-fingered leaf of a chaste tree in the palm, rubbing it lightly. Breathe deeply of its fragrance. Then, who knows?

Staying Power: Ruellias

> More and more I am coming to the conclusion that rain
> is a far more important consideration to gardens than sun.
> — Margaret Waterfield, 1907

After many years of drought, the record rains in North Central Texas during summer 2007 got everyone's attention. Swollen rivers, lakes, and streams displaced people from their homes, threatened the safety of livestock, and caused damage to infrastructure. Storm water runoff, carrying massive quantities of unsightly silt and debris, forced some regulatory agencies to declare boat ramps and swimming areas unsafe and closed them to public activities. Day after day of gully washers held up public works projects, leaving contractors facing mud ponds that prevented access to work sites and shaking their heads at expensive machinery gone idle. No one had witnessed anything like it. Even oldtimers stood by astonished at what they saw.

County extension offices reported unprecedented numbers of callers needing advice about drought-tolerant plants that seemed to be drowning, fearing some plants in danger of dying from too much water. In our own gardens we lost Blackfoot daisy, calylophus, hollyhock, salvia, Texas sage, and almost lost a couple of specimen desert willows and a newly planted cedar elm to the heavy rainfall. These experiences prompted a closer look at our plant stock to identify those best equipped to survive such extreme and unusual conditions.

Of course, many well-established plants came through just fine, but among the standout survivors ruellias ranked high on the list. While drought tolerance may be counted among their chief desirable characteristics, the ruellias withstood the summer's crisis by displaying other qualities as well: they remained unaffected by poor drainage from supersaturated soils; they evidenced neither disease nor soil-borne fungus, they retained their deep green leaves, and they continued to flower despite lack of sun from a daily cloud cover. The only casualties were a few blossoms fallen away from a mother plant by the velocity of excessive downpours.

We have several species of ruellia in our gardens, their starts given to us by friends who declared, "Don't worry; you can't kill 'em. And be careful where you put 'em 'cause they'll take over." Indeed, the ruellias have proven themselves aggressive, spreading perennials, tolerant of poor soils, of sun or shade, drought, or overdoses of rain. Most have blue-violet or purple blossoms, but some are white or pink. They bloom beginning mid to late spring, often continuing until frost. Leaves fade and turn brown in winter, then return in the spring.

R. brittoniana, sometimes called Mexican petunia, the tallest of our ruellias, grows to some 24" to 30" high. These we planted for erosion control on a difficult hillside that receives no supplementary water, and very little care. Within a couple of years' time they have colonized approximately 2,000 square feet there, camouflaging unsightly spots and stabilizing a swale area where nothing else would grow. The sight of a mass planting of ruellia in early morning or late afternoon takes the breath away, the violet-blue blossoms positively luminous in the liquid light.

Our other ruellias are equally tough and handsome. *R. nudiflora*, sometimes called wild petunia is a Texas native and hosts butterfly larvae; *R. brittoniana*, or "Katie's" (so named for Houston nursery woman, the late Katy Ferguson) has long, narrow, dark green leaves that form thick rosettes, hugging the ground to make an excellent ground cover.

After the experiences of the 2007 summer deluge, I am inclined to agree with Margaret Waterfield on the importance of rain versus sun to gardens. But I would add that ruellias also are an important considera-tion—certainly for any Texas garden.

New Garden Visage: Plant Toxicity

Adding a puppy to our household caused intense experiences in the garden some years ago. Previous leisurely strolls, carefree or filled with idle enjoyment of the sights, smells, and feel of plants shifted instead to canine monitoring. As the puppy sniffed about, dug, pounced, chewed, or scythed her way pell-mell through what was left of the zinnias, her human atten-dants focused intently so as to protect her, and the plants, from harm. Then it was the puppy that indulged in carefree enjoyment of the place.

This new garden experience with canine influence prompted us to begin looking at plants for their potential toxicity. A Web search furnished an informative list of poisonous plants grouped by type: house plants, flower garden plants, vegetable garden plants, ornamental plants, trees and shrubs, plants in wooded areas, plants in swamps or moist areas, and plants in fields. The information offered here extended to details such as toxic parts and the ensuing telltale symptoms.

A glance through the list produced shock waves of realization that many plants in our garden might cause problems for the puppy. Even taking into account that what can be toxic to humans might not necessarily be as harmful to animals, the list seemed daunting: hyacinth, narcissus, daffodil, oleander, larkspur, autumn crocus, Star of Bethlehem, lily-of-the-valley, iris, wisteria, laurels, oaks, and mistletoe comprise a partial list. Of the group, mistletoe and oleander alarmed us most. Mistletoe berries are fatal, the website says, stating that "both children and adults have died from eating the berries."

Mistletoe berries posed a particular concern for us here. In years past, there being no children or pets regularly present on the property, we could vigorously harvest the mistletoe in our trees for holiday decoration, allowing the translucent berries to fall where they may. The challenge with the puppy around was to remove the mistletoe *and* the berries. Raking, sweeping, even vacuuming the berries leapt to mind. As to oleander, the website made the following disturbing comment:

> Who would expect that the beautiful oleander bush—grown indoors and outdoors all over the country—contains a deadly heart stimulant, similar to the drug digitalis? So powerful is this poison that a single leaf of an oleander can kill a child. And, many people have died merely from eating steaks speared on oleander twigs and roasted over a fire.

The question of what to do about our specimen oleander was especially troublesome. Grown from a cutting given to me by my mother, we had nursed it through viral attacks, drought, hailstorms, and freeze damage until it eventually matured to become a seven-foot tall, showy ornamental that helped to camouflage the compost heap directly behind. Its profusion of bright, fuchsia-colored blossoms stood pert and erect, with stems and flowers lasting days and days when brought indoors for display in a favored vase. But as there was no effective way to block access to the shrub or prevent leaves from blowing into the dog's water bowl, we regretfully cut the oleander and removed every scrap of leaf, stem, branch, or flower. A brutal act, to restore a little peace of mind.

Plants and flowers generally are assumed to be benign, filling garden or home with peace and beauty. Yet appearances can be deceiving, for many plants can have a darker side. Sixteenth-century English herbalist John Gerard clearly understood these aspects of plants in the garden when he wrote that some "are so beautiful, that a man would thinke they were of some excellent vertue, but *non est semper fides habenda fronti*" [there is no trusting to appearances].

Final Words

Gardening in Texas poses particular challenges. It also offers certain privileges in the form of its longer growing and flowering seasons.

A garden represents more than a mere collection of plants. It is a place of peace and tranquility in an ever changing world. A garden promises the future. And a garden makes us smile.

This has been a love story about gardening.

Dominique Cranmer Inge

Suggested Readings

The volumes consulted most frequently for these essays form a part of my personal garden library:

Botanica, Rev. Ed. Edition. Barnes and Noble publisher, 2001.

The American Horticultural Society Dictionary of Gardening. Doring Kindersley publisher, 1993.

The New Royal Horticultural Society Dictionary of Gardening. 4 vols. 1992 edition, Macmillan Press Limited, 1992.

Shinner's and Mahler's Illustrated Flora of North Central Texas. Eds. George M. Diggs, Jr. , Barney L. Lipscomb, and Robert J. O'Kennon. (A collaborative project of the Austin College Center for Environmental Studies and the Botanical Research Institute of Texas. BRIT, 1999.

Trees, Shrubs, and Woody Vines of the Southwest. Robert A. Vines. University of Texas Press, 1990.

The following books enlighten and add experiences of personal gardening triumphs, failures, and above all, they share the love of gardening:

Adventures with a Texas Nauralist. Roy Bedichek. U of Texas Press, 1988.

The Wild Braid. Stanley Kunitz. Norton, 2005.

Beds I Have Known: Confessions of a Passionate Amateur Gardener Martha Smith. Fireside, 1990.

The Quotable Gardener. Ed. Charles Elliott, Metro Book, new ed. 2000.

Essays of E. B. White, E. B. White. Harper Perennial Modern Classics, 2006.

Making More Plants: The Science, Art, and Joy of Propagation. Ken Druse. Clarkson Potter/Crown, 2001.

Book Club Discussion Questions

1. Has reading this book changed your general approach to gardening? Explain by giving specific examples.

2. Of the plants discussed in the book, which one do you now feel most different about as a result of the author's treatment of the plant. Explain your answer with specifics.

3. "Salute to a Volunteer: Clammyweed" describes a case of mistaken identity. Compare this mistake with a similar experience you have had with a plant.

4. Chapter 4 describes seasons in the garden. Name your favorite season and compare your thoughts about this season with what you find in Chapter 4.

5. How is the epigraph relevant to the book?

6. Do you find the author's relationship to gardening meditative, physical, cerebral or some combination of these? Cite evidence from the book to support your answer.

7. The editors have described the chapters in the book as partly literary and partly scientific. Giving reasons for your choices, select the one that is most literary and the one that is most scientific.

8. Elements of humor appear in the book. Find three examples and suggest reasons for the author's choosing to include the humor.

9. The subsections of Chapter 9 might be described as mood pieces. Compare them and explain which ones best evoke mood.

10. Explain the significance of the book's subtitle. What literary allusion(s) does it make?

About The Author

Dominique Cranmer Inge grew up in a bilingual household speaking French to her French mother and Southern English to her American father. The formative years she spent in French North Africa, southern France, and Atlanta, Georgia instilled a lifelong interest in the language arts and an appreciation for differing landscapes. She received a B. A. in English from Georgia State University and her M. A. in art history from Southern Methodist University. She has worked for major art museums in Atlanta and Dallas.

In 1990 Dominique and her husband, Charles Inge, purchased a lakefront property in Granbury, Texas and began to develop their hillside organic gardens. Their antique roses and organic methods were featured in the PBS television series *The New Garden* hosted by Liz Druitt, and photographed for Druitt's book *Organic Roses*. Photos of their thornless roses have appeared in *Southern Living*.

For thirteen years Dominique wrote a bimonthly column "Notes from the Brazos" for Judy Barrett's Texas organic gardening news magazine *Homegrown: Good Sense Organic Gardening* now collected for this book. Her freelance cover stories appeared in *Texas Highways* and *Hood & Somervell Today* magazines, and she has contributed to *Horticulture* magazine, *The New Garden Journal, Granbury Showcase Magazine,* and several anthologies. She is a member of the editorial advisory board of the *Langdon Review of the Arts in Texas,* an annual anthology published by Tarleton State University.

Dominique lives with her husband at their Brazos House property in Granbury, Texas.

A Redbud in Mid March

www.ingramcontent.com/pod-product-compliance
Lightning Source LLC
Chambersburg PA
CBHW060052100426
42742CB00014B/2797